Unhinged: Restoring Sanity to End Times Teaching © 2025 by David Campbell

All rights reserved. No part of this publication may be reproduced, distributed, or transmitted in any form or by any means, including photocopying, recording, or other electronic or mechanical methods, without the prior written permission of the publisher or author, except in the case of brief quotations embodied in critical reviews and certain other noncommercial uses permitted by copyright law. For permission requests, email the publisher or author at addresses below:

Contact the author:
www.davidhcampbell.com

Contact the publisher:
David Campbell Christian Publishing
trinitycc@rogers.com

Scripture quotations are from the ESV® Bible (The Holy Bible, English Standard Version®), copyright © 2001 by Crossway, a publishing ministry of Good News Publishers. Used by permission. All rights reserved.

ISBN-978-1-0693289-4-6

Printed in the United States of America
Ingram Printing & Distribution, 2025

First Edition

UNHINGED

RESTORING SANITY TO END TIMES TEACHING

DAVID CAMPBELL

Dedicated with gratitude and respect to

Dr. G.K. Beale

without whose teaching I would know little about eschatology

	FOREWORD
ONE	What's behind Left Behind?
TWO	What is dispensationalism?
THREE	The rapture
FOUR	The last days
FIVE	The sign of the Lord's coming
SIX	The two witnesses
SEVEN	The apostasy and the rise of the antichrist
EIGHT	The restrainer
NINE	The last conflict and the fall of the antichrist
TEN	The mark of the beast
ELEVEN	The plagues
TWELVE	666
THIRTEEN	144,000
FOURTEEN	Armageddon
FIFTEEN	Is the church in the book of Revelation?
SIXTEEN	The tribulation
SEVENTEEN	The millennium
EIGHTEEN	Gog, Magog and the final battle
NINETEEN	Israel and the Jewish people in God's plan
	ABOUT THE AUTHOR

FOREWORD

This is the third in a series of books I have written on Biblical eschatology. The subject matter of the first two, Mystery Explained: A Simple Guide to Revelation and Israel and the Land Promise in Biblical Prophecy, is clear enough from their titles.

The aim of this book is to provide a concise topical summary of all the major issues that generally come up in discussions of eschatology, and has been informed by years of questions thrown in my direction in countless settings. It may be surprising to some people that a number of these topics fall outside the scope of the book of Revelation, which is part of the reason why I've written this study.

I am grateful for the financial assistance of Calvary Church Miami and Pastor Alex Sagot in underwriting production of this book. Thanks also to Pastor Evan Sustar for once again providing his excellent proofreading skills, though I take responsibility for any remaining errors in the text. Thanks to Pastor David Baker for contributing the idea behind the title to this book. And as always my gratitude to Owen Woltjer and his team at davidandbrook.com for producing the book to their usual high standard.

As always, I am indebted most of all to the patience and support of my wife Elaine, who has endured countless hours of listening to me speak on eschatology-related subjects, and in the process has become pretty knowledgeable herself.

May God be glorified and his people edified through this book.

Soli Deo gloria — glory to God alone.

CHAPTER ONE

WHAT'S BEHIND LEFT BEHIND?

A friend at seminary made the remark, "Your eschatology affects everything you believe." At the time I brushed his comment off. No longer. Here's why my view has changed. The New Testament consistently asserts that the last days began with the earthly ministry of Jesus and the launch of the church at Pentecost. If you believe that the last days are a brief period immediately before the return of Christ, you will not be able to understand fully the meaning of the Christian life now.

The New Testament consistently asserts that all Old Testament prophecies regarding God's plan for the future, including God's promises to Abraham, are fulfilled in Christ, not in the state of Israel or a future covenant with the Jewish people outside of Christ. If you believe that the main prophetic program of God deals with Israel, you will fail to understand fully the meaning of God's purposes for the church.

The New Testament consistently asserts that wars and political conflicts, famines, pestilence, and natural disasters will occur throughout the church age and are not in themselves signs of the end. If you believe that such phenomena are a sign of the end, you will spend most of your time fixated on the latest news reports from the middle east and other peripheral items, you will become fear-focussed, not faith-focussed, and you will miss what God is really doing on the earth.

Now do you begin to see how your eschatology, or even your lack of eschatology, affects everything you believe and even how you live?

How did we get into this mess?

The early years of the nineteenth century saw an increase in expectation that the return of the Lord was soon, if not imminent. Occasional upsurges in apocalyptic expectations have occurred throughout church history, notably around the time of the turn of the first millennium. Some also began at that time to advance the idea that a sign of this return would be the return of the Jewish people to their ancestral homeland. It was within this historical context that a preacher called Edward Irving, who had developed an interest in the fulfillment of Bible prophecy, began in 1826 to preach the imminent return of Christ, which he believed would occur in 1868. Irving declared himself the latter-day John the Baptist in his role of the one called to prepare for the Lord's soon coming. In 1830, a young teenaged woman in Scotland called Margaret MacDonald, who was a follower of Irving, had an ecstatic vision in an Irvingite prayer meeting concerning the events leading up to the return of Christ. She wrote these words: "Only those who have the light of God within them will see the sign of his appearance… 'tis only those that are alive in him that will be caught up to meet him in the air." These words were interpreted to refer to a previously-unknown *secret* return of Christ, visible only to believers.

Meanwhile in 1828, another British Bible teacher, John Nelson Darby, a regular participant in Irving's gatherings, began to hold his own prophetic conferences. Like a number of others in the decades preceding him, Darby believed that the re-establishment of Israel as a nation would be a sign of the Lord's imminent return, and he began preaching this in 1829. But Darby went much, much further. Contrary to eighteen centuries of Christian teaching, Darby taught that the kingdom of God preached by Christ had nothing to do with the church, was earthly and material in nature, and would be fulfilled in a series of events commencing in the restoration of the state of Israel. He developed a system of Biblical interpretation called dispensationalism. This system arbitrarily, and without clear support from the Biblical text, divides history into seven "dispensations" or ages in which God relates to people differently.

Theologians have always perceived that God has dealt in different ways throughout history, yet have also understood that he has always done so in a consistent manner which carefully develops his plan of salvation by grace. The sacrificial system, for instance, was designed to be a prophetic foreshadowing of the sacrifice of his Son. From the promise of Genesis 3 regarding the crushing of the serpent's head to the provision of a lamb to Abraham on Mount Moriah, though Moses and the law, and all the way to the cross, there is but one coherent plan — one covenant of grace.

But Darby cut the dealings of God up into separate and somewhat disconnected pieces. Although Darby taught there were seven dispensations from creation to the millennium, the two most important were those in which God relates to Israel and to the church. According to Darby's new system, the Old Testament was written exclusively for the Jews, and its prophetic promises are for Israel alone. In fact, the main point of all God's earthly dealings with humanity was the fulfillment of his covenant with the Jewish people. The new covenant of Jeremiah 31 will not be fulfilled until the earthly millennium, and only then with the Jewish people. That is when the work of Christ will finally prove effective. In spite of the words of Jesus at the Last Supper and the clear application of Jeremiah 31 to the church in Hebrews 8,

Darby (and dispensationalist theologians since him like C.I. Scofield, Lewis Sperry Chafer and John Walvoord) taught that the church *does not participate* in the new covenant. *The meaning of the dispensation of grace in which we now live is that God chooses to be gracious to the church only in light of the future blessings coming to Israel.*

At the heart of Darby's teaching was the idea that the purpose for which God sent Jesus was the establishment of an earthly Jewish messianic kingdom based in Jerusalem. Christ failed in his mission, so to speak, when the Jews crucified him instead of receiving him as king. God then had to revert to a different plan, which was the resurrection, the sending of the Spirit and the birth of the Gentile church. According to Darby and his modern followers such as Chafer and Walvoord, the church is Plan B, a mere "parenthesis" in the real purpose of God, which is to fulfill his original covenant with Israel.

But Darby had one massive problem. Whereas Christian theology had always seen the plan of God unfolding in a consistent manner, Darby saw God operating in a number of watertight and very different compartments. According to his teaching, God could only operate in one dispensation at any given time. Having taught that God had established the church in the dispensation of grace, Darby had no Biblical way of explaining how God could get back to his original intention. The existence of the church on earth prevented the resumption of God's covenant dealings with the Jews.

Enter Margaret MacDonald. Because of his close ties with Edward Irving, Darby knew who she was, and had heard of her extraordinary prophecy. In it, and in spite of his teaching that the sign gifts had ceased with the writing of the New Testament in the apostolic era, he found the answer to his predicament. Within months of Margaret's vision, Darby began teaching her revelation of the secret return of Christ, something never before envisioned in the 1800-year history of the church. Margaret had seen the vision, but Darby provided its interpretation. *The purpose of the secret return was the removal of the church.* Between 1831 and 1833, Darby held a series of prophetic conferences, attended and endorsed by his friend Edward Irving, in which he outlined for the first time his revelation of a secret return of Christ. The vision had handed Darby the answer to his riddle. The secret return, which Darby called the "rapture," was to remove the church from the world, thus enabling God to return to his original plan of establishing his covenant with the Jews.

One event, of course, was needed to set this chain of events into motion: the restoration of the state of Israel in fulfillment of Biblical prophecy. Darby was just as obsessed as his friend Irving was with this event. This for Darby would start the last days prophetic clock, for Jesus had taught that "this generation," which Darby interpreted to be *those Christians alive at the establishment of the state of Israel*, would live to see the rapture. Once the church had been raptured, there would follow a seven-year period of tribulation culminating in the battle of Armageddon portrayed in Rev.16:14-16. This battle would involve a coalition of pagan nations attacking the restored state of Israel. These events would precipitate a mass conversion of Jews, and following Armageddon, Christ would establish an earthly kingdom based in Jerusalem, consisting of Jews converted in the tribulation. Darby identified this as the millennial period referred to in Rev. 20:1-3, and saw it lasting a literal thousand years.

Darby's ideas spread, but not within orthodox Christianity. In the early 1840s, William Miller, co-founder of the Seventh Day Adventists, predicted that Christ would visibly return in 1844. When this did not happen, he declared that Christ had *invisibly and secretly* entered the heavenly sanctuary to commence the process of eternal judgment. Mormonism, birthed at about the same time, while not accepting the secret rapture, endorsed Darby's concept of a literal earthly millennium.

But perhaps the most far-reaching and disastrous consequence of Darby's teaching was its impact on Charles Taze Russell. Russell was heavily influenced by the Seventh Day Adventists in their adoption of Darby's rapture, as well as their rejection of the Trinity and of a literal hell. Like Darby, he was an ardent Zionist, believing in the re-establishment of the state of Israel as the key to the return of Christ. And so he established an organization called Zion's Watch Tower Tract Society — now known as the Jehovah's Witnesses. Russell declared that Darby's rapture would occur in 1878, and in preparation sold all his businesses. Later, when this failed to take place, he published books in which he asserted that Christ had in fact *secretly and invisibly* returned in 1874 to begin the end-times harvest through the Jehovah's Witnesses. He borrowed Darby's idea of the seven-year tribulation ending in a multinational attack on a restored Israel culminating in the battle of Armageddon. Russell saw the outbreak of World War I as marking the end of the Gentile age, the beginning of Armageddon and the establishment of the state of Israel. He taught that Jews did not need to be converted, should return to Palestine and there reconstitute the Biblical state of Israel, which would henceforth be the center of God's earthly kingdom. Russell also adopted Darby's ideas of dispensations. He later declared that the kingdom of God was established in heaven in 1914, to be governed by a group of 144,000 heavenly-resurrected chosen Witnesses who would work in heaven toward establishment of a millennial paradise on earth. While Russell's views do not cohere exactly with Darby's, the numerous parallels make clear his dependency on Darby's thought.

Dispensationalism was popularized with the publication of a study Bible by C.I. Scofield, an associate of D.L. Moody, in 1909. It burst into prominence further with the apparent vindication of Darby's prophecy concerning the restoration of the state of Israel in 1948, thus setting off Darby's prophetic clock. Its view of the rapture, the seven-year tribulation, the rebuilding of the temple, the re-institution of the sacrificial system, and the literal thousand-year millennial kingdom were entrenched by the prominence of dispensational institutions such as Dallas Theological Seminary and Moody Bible Institute, the works of Lewis Sperry Chafer and John Walvoord, the best-selling book *The Late Great Planet Earth* by Hal Lindsey, and the *Left Behind* novels and films of Tim LaHaye and Jerry Jenkins.

Today, this understanding of eschatology is the prevailing view among Christians in North America, even if few have comprehension of its details and consequences. Many, possibly most of you reading this book have, knowingly or not, allowed your understanding of the end-times to be conditioned by it.If that is the case, you need to know the shaky foundations of what you have mistakenly accepted as Biblical truth.

CHAPTER TWO

WHAT IS DISPENSATIONALISM?

Let's do a quick recap of the previous chapter and then proceed further.

According to dispensational teaching, the key to the fulfillment of all Biblical prophecy regarding the end times is the re-establishment of the state of Israel, which occurred in 1948. This restoration was necessary in order for the prophetic clock to begin its countdown, culminating in the rapture and the events of the seven-year tribulation, at the heart of which is an attack on the restored state of Israel by a coalition of nations led by the Antichrist. This in turn paves the way for the battle of Armageddon, the second, visible return of Christ, the re-establishment of the earthly kingdom promised to King David, and the restoration of the Jerusalem temple, the Levitical order, the Aaronic priesthood and the sacrificial system, all of which is presided over by Christ in an earthly millennial rule based in Jerusalem. God's intention in sending Christ to earth was to fulfill God's promise to David that his descendants would rule over an earthly kingdom. Unexpectedly, the Jewish people rejected God's offer and crucified the Messiah instead. God was now faced with a problem. He resorted to Plan B. He raised Jesus from the dead, and created the church.

The church was not God's original purpose, but exists as a "parenthesis" in the divine plan, a plan which is centered on Israel. God is thus left with two distinct peoples, and must deal separately with each. The dispensations cannot overlap. God must now fulfill his original plan to establish an earthly kingdom ruled over by Christ. In order to maintain the distinction between his two peoples, he must remove the church from the equation. This occurs through a secret return of Christ, visible only to the church, called the "rapture." The rapture, the teaching continues, precipitates the seven year tribulation allegedly prophesied in Dan. 9:24-27 and referred to in Rev. 7:14 as "the great tribulation."

The church, in fact, is a people without a covenant. The Old Testament was written exclusively for the Jews, and is of no relevance to Christians. Its prophetic promises are intended for Israel, not the church. Even the prophesied new covenant of Jeremiah 31, which Hebrews 8 applies clearly to the finished work of Christ and its benefits for Christian believers, is for Jews only. This means that *the church has no operating covenant with God.* God chooses to deal with the church by grace in view of the fact his prophesied new covenant with the Jews will come into effect during the millennium. The church, in effect, receives an early installment of God's blessing on Israel, though that blessing, *including the finished work of Christ*, does not properly belong to the church. *The church relates to Christ only indirectly, by grace, through the medium of God's future millennial blessing of Israel.*

The restoration of the state of Israel is presumed to have taken place before the visionary section of Revelation unfolds at 4:1. The events of the seven year tribulation, according to Darby and his followers, are described in Revelation chapters 6 through 19. During this time, a personal antichrist will arise. At first he appears friendly to Israel and in fact rebuilds the ancient temple. But then he betrays the alliance, and turns his attention to Israel's destruction, thus precipitating the destruction of the temple as prophesied by Jesus. In the ensuing period of crisis, many of the Jewish people will be converted to faith in Christ. At the end of the tribulation, Christ will return again, this time visibly, and destroy the forces of the antichrist at Armageddon.

Following Armageddon, Christ will establish an earthly, thousand-year rule from Jerusalem to fulfill God's original intention. Jews (and some Gentiles) saved in the tribulation will enter this kingdom, and will live very long and healthy lives, many surviving right through until the end of the millennium. At the beginning of the millennial period, only believers will live on the earth, the unsaved being held in Hades until the final judgment following the thousand years. Some dispensationalists suggest it is possible that those who do die in the millennium may be instantly resurrected and gain immortal bodies, existing alongside those still mortal. Raptured saints in glorified bodies meanwhile reside in the new Jerusalem, which will hover above the earth and be visible to it, but will also from time to time come down and mingle with the mortal inhabitants of the earth. Worship will be conducted from the now-restored temple. The Levitical priesthood and offerings will be re-instituted as the means of worshiping God. At the end of the thousand years, a further rebellion will take place, described in Rev. 20:7-10. This will be led, it is conjectured, by the unsaved descendants of millennial believers (as only saved people entered the millennium). Christ will defeat the rebels and merge his two peoples into the eternal new Jerusalem. The resurrection of the dead will at last take place, the raptured church and the millennial Jews will be reunited, and the lost will be taken from Hades and cast into the lake of fire.

Let's take four major claims of dispensationalism and respond to them.

Claim number one: The church has no covenant with God.

Response: This claim makes a farce of what Jesus taught at the Lord's Supper concerning the covenant in his blood. His teaching assumes that this covenant is about to be initiated through his death and resurrection, and applied to all those who believe in him. It likewise rejects the explicit citation of Jeremiah 31 in Hebrews 8:7-13 and 10:15-18, words which are written to Christian believers and assumed to have been already fulfilled through the work of Christ, as the entirety of the letter makes clear. The verses following in chapter 10 (19-25) make abundantly clear that the blessings of Jeremiah's prophesied new covenant *are already operating* in the lives of those to whom the letter is written. It stretches credulity to believe, as some dispensationalists suggest, that Hebrews was written to an entirely Jewish congregation, especially as Paul's Gentile associate Timothy is mentioned as having a role in the congregation's life (13:23), and the letter was written either from Rome or to the church at Rome (13:24). The congregation is addressed as the "saints" (13:24), a term which in the New Testament universally refers to Christian believers.

Claim number two: The key to the fulfillment of all Biblical prophecy concerning the end times is the re-establishment of the state of Israel in 1948. Although some Messianic promises were fulfilled in Christ's own ministry (which itself was exclusively to the Jews), God's *end-times* promises in the Old Testament are directed toward Israel, and will culminate in the millennium in the triumphant establishment of an earthly kingdom led from Jerusalem by a descendant of David.

Response: The Bible teaches that all Old Testament prophecies are fulfilled in and through Christ and Christ alone. This is especially true of the Jewish feasts. Christ is the new temple (Jn. 2:13-22; 4:21-26). He fulfills the Sabbath (Mt. 12:1-8), the Passover (Jn. 19:36), the Day of Atonement (Isa. 52:13-53:12) and the Feast of Tabernacles, which promised the outpouring of the Holy Spirit (Jn. 7:37-44). Christ is the new Bethel (Jn. 1:51), the promised Messianic wine (Jer. 31:12; Jn. 2:1-12), and the new manna (Jn. 6:1-15, 30-34). He is the prophesied giver of abundant water and the Spirit (Ezek. 36:25-27; Jn. 3:1-15). He is the new Moses (Ac. 3:22-26), who calms the sea and walks on the water (Jn. 6:16-21). The entire Old Testament in its prophecy and typology points to Christ. If Israel was God's disobedient son (Hos. 11:1-2), Jesus is the faithful, true and unique Son (Mt. 2:15; Jn. 1:14). He is therefore also the true Israel, in that all God's promises for the nation are fulfilled in his life, death, resurrection, exaltation, seating at God's right hand and second coming. *This principle is necessarily extended to his body, the church.* This is why Jesus and his body, the church, constitute the true Israel, fulfilling the promise given to Moses, "You shall be to me a kingdom of priests and a holy nation" (Exod. 19:6), a promise explicitly applied to the church in 1 Pet. 2:9; Rev. 1:6; 5:10. Jesus, the Son of David, fulfilled the promises made to David concerning an eternal kingdom. This kingdom was initiated by Jesus in his earthly ministry, as is made clear by his constant announcing of its presence (Mt. 3:17, 23; 6:33; 10:7; 11:12; 12:28; 16:19), and will come in its consummation at his return. *This is not what dispensationalists disparagingly call "replacement theology," as if the church simply replaces Israel.* Rather, the truth is that Christ himself fulfills and embodies Israel, *and in his person receives all the promises made to Israel. T*hose who are in Christ, whether Jews or Gentiles, receive those promises by virtue of their relationship with him.

Claim number three: God sent Christ to earth to establish an earthly kingdom in Jerusalem and to rule as the fulfillment of God's promise to David. The Jewish people rejected God's offer and crucified the Messiah instead. God was now faced with a problem. He resorted to Plan B. He raised Jesus from the dead and created the church. The church is not his primary focus, but exists as a "parenthesis" in the divine plan, which is centered instead on Israel. God thus has two peoples and deals separately with each of them.

Response: God sent Jesus into the world for one reason only: to suffer and die for our sins on the cross (Isa. 52:13-53:12; Psalm 22). God has infinite foreknowledge, and his plan from all eternity was to send Christ to earth to create *one new people* out of Jew and Gentile alike (Eph. 1:3-10; 2:11-22). He did this in order to fulfill the promise given to Abraham that through his offspring *all the nations* of the earth would be blessed (Gen. 22:18). God has only one covenant people, his church. Believing Jews are incorporated along with Gentiles into the one body of Christ (Gal. 3:28-29; Eph. 4:6). The earthly Jerusalem, physical Israel, is in slavery, and is contrasted by Paul with the heavenly Jerusalem, the church, which is free (Gal. 4:21-31). Believing Jews represent the faithful remnant saved through faith in Christ and added to the church (Rom. (9:6-13; 11:23-32). The church is the climax of God's prophetic plan in Christ (Eph. 3:7-13).

Claim number four: Following Armageddon, Christ will establish his earthly thousand year rule from Jerusalem and thus fulfill God's original intention for sending him. Jews saved in the tribulation will enter it and live very long lives, quite possibly surviving right through until the end of the millennium. Those who do die may be instantly resurrected and gain immortal bodies. Raptured saints in glorified bodies meanwhile reside in the new Jerusalem, which will hover above the earth, but will also mingle with the earth's mortal inhabitants. Worship will be conducted from the restored temple. The Levitical priesthood and offerings will be re-instituted as the means of worshiping God. At the end of the millennium, there will occur a further rebellion led by unsaved children of millennial believers. Christ will defeat them and merge his two peoples into the eternal new Jerusalem.

Response: The description of the battle in Rev. 20:7-10, which occurs at the end of the millennium, shows that it is identical to the battle of Armageddon, described in chapters

16 and 19, as the same Scriptures from Ezekiel and Zechariah are utilized in all three passages. On every eschatological view, Armageddon occurs *at the end* of the church age. This shows that the millennium, which occurs *prior to* the battle of 20:7-10, is identical to the church age. The Bible teaches only one, visible return of Christ. The Bible teaches only one resurrection of the dead. The Bible teaches that the sacrifices of the law are once and for all done away with by the sacrifice of Christ (Hebrews 7-11). Dispensationalism wrongly teaches that (1) the curse of death on humanity and on the natural creation will continue after Christ's second coming; (2) unbelievers will have the opportunity of coming to Christ after his second coming; and (3) unbelievers will not be resurrected or judged until 1000 years after Christ's second coming. Such teachings are completely contrary to what is taught anywhere in the New Testament.

The prophetic clock and the return of Christ

Dispensationalism, as we have noted, is built around one significant event: the restoration of the state of Israel in 1948, because this represents the necessary basis for the fulfillment of God's covenant with the Jewish people. Without Israel, nothing else in Darby's scheme is possible. And so this event is seen as setting off what dispensationalists call the prophetic clock, based on their interpretation of Matthew 24. We explain our understanding of that chapter later in this book, but here is a summary statement. In response to a comment from the disciples, Jesus told them that the buildings of the temple they were looking at would be destroyed (verse 1), and later added, "this generation will not pass away until all these things take place" (verse 34). His prophecy, on our view, was fulfilled when the Romans destroyed that temple in AD 70, which could reasonably have occurred during the lifetime of some, if not most of the disciples. Dispensationalists, however, believe the passage deals with the events of the very last days. The temple to be destroyed is not the temple the disciples were actually asking about but, completely unbeknownst to them, it is the temple rebuilt by the antichrist more than two thousand years later during the first half of the seven year tribulation, and destroyed by him in the second half of that period. The identity of "this generation" cannot then be that of the original disciples, but rather refers to a group of Jewish people living in the very end times. This group is then arbitrarily defined as those Jews living at the time of the restoration of the state of Israel in 1948. *That is to say, many if not most of that group of people will live to see the rapture, the tribulation and the visible return of Christ.* Ever since 1948, dispensationalist teachers have been brimming over with predictions of attacks on Israel, the appearance of the antichrist and the rapture. All of them have been proven wrong, but they keep on coming. The math, however, is working against them. At the time of writing of this book — 2025 — *seventy-seven years have passed* since the founding of the state of Israel. If the events referred to by "all these things" include the rapture, the tribulation, and the visible return of Christ, *another seven years must be added* to account for the period following the rapture. Dispensational teachers have been forced to keep expanding their definition of a "generation" far beyond what would have been the norm in Biblical times, and are now beginning to move beyond the limits of what would be considered a normal lifespan in our times. The truth is that the vast majority of Jewish people alive in 1948 are now dead. The *youngest*, at time of this writing, is nearing 80.

One of the main downfalls of Darby's system is the way it assumes a scenario of end-times events and then writes those events into the Biblical text, even when the text itself says something completely different. The basis for interpreting Biblical eschatology, and particularly Revelation, as we will see again and again, is the rich treasury of Old Testament allusions, not the latest news reports from the middle east.

CHAPTER THREE

THE RAPTURE

Understanding the historical origins of the doctrine of the secret return of Christ should immediately raise a red flag about accepting it. But can we prove it wrong from the Bible? The answer is yes.

It's in the two letters to the Thessalonians that Paul is most specific about the events surrounding the Lord's return, and where he most closely echoes the teachings of Jesus on the same subject. 1 Thessalonians 4 is where Darby went to provide a Biblical justification for his novel doctrine of the rapture. This chapter is therefore critical for understanding correctly what Paul taught about the return of Christ.

Here the apostle's goal is to clear up confusion in the

Thessalonian church as to the nature and order of events preceding the Lord's return. He describes the future "coming" of the Lord and our "meeting" him as he descends in the clouds. What does he mean by these two terms, and what does he mean when he speaks of our being "caught up in the clouds" to meet the Lord? These are the questions we must answer.

The parousia: the coming of the Lord

"For what is our hope or joy or crown of boasting before our Lord Jesus at his coming? Is it not you?" (1 Thess. 2:19).

The word "coming" in this and other texts in the New Testament is the Greek word *parousia*. Paul uses this word a number of times to refer to Jesus' second coming (1 Cor. 15:23; 1 Thess. 2:19; 3:13; 4:15; 5:23; 2 Thess. 2:1, 8). The same word is used to refer to the Lord's coming by the disciples (Mt. 24:3); by Jesus himself (Mt. 24:3, 27, 37, 39); by James (Jas. 5:5, 8); by Peter (2 Pet. 1:16; 3:4, 12); and by John (1 Jn. 2:28). It's the key New Testament word for the second coming of Christ.

So this is a highly significant word in terms of understanding the Lord's return. Providentially, we have some very specific information about what it means and why the New Testament uses it so widely. *Parousia* was a technical term which referred to the coming of kings or high-ranking officials to a city or locality for an official visit. A delegation of prominent citizens would go outside the city and meet the ruler at his *parousia* for the purpose of escorting him back into the city, where he was duly honored and his rule proclaimed. Following this, he took his seat on the throne to pronounce judgment, acquitting the innocent and convicting the guilty. This was a very common custom in the Greek and Roman world, and the Thessalonians would have known exactly what Paul meant by it. It may well have been why Paul was accused at Thessalonica of saying that there is another king, Jesus (Ac. 17:7).

So when Paul uses the word *parousia* here, he is describing an event in which Christ returns to rule over his renewed earthly kingdom, *not an event in which he takes believers out of this world* while leaving it in the hands of the devil. The picture is of believers going outside the city to meet the Lord as he approaches, and then taking him back into the city, where his rulership will be proclaimed over the renewed earth and heavens, and where he will sit down on his throne to pass judgment on the saved and the lost. The *parousia* is therefore the *immediate precursor* to the great white throne judgment, and is not separated from it by a thousand year gap.

Jesus himself prophetically foreshadowed the *parousia* on Palm Sunday, where his followers went outside the city as he approached in order to escort him back into the city and honor him as their Lord.

Caught up in the clouds: return not rapture (1 Thess. 4:13-18)

1 Thess. 4:15-17: "For this we declare to you by a word from the Lord, that we who are alive, who are left until the coming of the Lord, will not precede those who have fallen asleep. For the Lord himself will descend from heaven with a cry of command, with the voice of an archangel, and with the sound of the trumpet of God. And the dead in Christ will rise first. Then we who are alive, who are left, will be caught up together with them in the clouds to meet the Lord in the air, and so we will always be with the Lord."

The church in Thessalonica was one of the churches Paul founded on his first missionary journey in the year AD 48 (Ac. 17:1-9). He stayed in the city only three weeks before persecution forced him to move on, so he had been unable to lay down doctrinal foundations in the way he did in cities like Ephesus and Corinth, where he was able to stay much longer. In the months following Paul's departure, it appears — not surprisingly — that some members of the congregation had died. The believers had become alarmed by a false teaching that those who die before the Lord's return would somehow miss out on the events of that great day. Perhaps they had assumed incorrectly that all believers would live to see it. In order to address this concern, Paul gives assurance in these verses that those who have died in the Lord will be raised from the dead in time for them, and those still alive, to meet the Lord together at his coming. No one will be left out. Verse 15 is the third time in the letter (after 2:19 and 3:13) that Paul has used the word *parousia*. As we've seen, this refers to Christ's appearance on his way into the recreated world to establish his rule and take his place of judgment. Paul is concerned in this passage to establish correct understanding of his teaching concerning the Lord's coming by adding more definition to his description of the event. In verses 15-17, we have in fact the most explicit description of the Lord's return anywhere in his writings. Paul sets forth clearly the order of events.

First, the Lord descends from heaven. He does so with a commanding shout, the voice of an archangel and the sound of a trumpet. The shout (*keleusma*) was an authoritative cry given at a moment of great importance. The archangel is almost certainly Michael (Jude verse 9), the only archangel mentioned in the New Testament. Lending support to this idea is that fact that Michael appears in Dn. 10:13 and 12:1 as the "patron saint" or divine protector of God's people, and is also mentioned in Rev. 12:7 in that same capacity. Revelation, as well as many other parts of the New Testament (Mt. 13:39; Mk. 8:38; 1 Cor. 6:3; 2 Thess. 1:7) contains references to angelic figures at the return of the Lord. The sounding of the trumpet, which in the Old Testament acted as a signal that something important was about to happen, is also often connected in the New Testament with the Lord's return (Mt. 24:31; 1 Cor. 15:52; and various places in Revelation).

Second, deceased believers are resurrected. The problem for the Thessalonians is not that they feared not rising at all. They would surely have been taught by Paul concerning the resurrection of the dead and eternal life as part of his basic gospel message (1 Thess. 1:10). The fear they apparently had was that believers who had died since Paul had brought the gospel to them might miss out on participating in the glorious events surrounding Christ's return, and would only be resurrected following that. That is why Paul does not insist on the fact that deceased believers will rise, but rather on the fact they will *rise first.*

Third, the resurrected saints and living believers are caught up in the air to meet the Lord as he returns. The critical question here is the meaning of the phrase "caught up." The Greek verb is *harpazo*, and its Latin translation is *rapio*, which takes the form *raptum* as a participle, from which we get the word "rapture." Does this text really speak (as Darby claimed) of a removing of the saints from this world and a leaving behind of the lost? The first problem we face with this view is simple. How could the Thessalonians possibly have known anything about a secret rapture, in which Christ returns surreptitiously to remove the church, when Paul had *only previously taught them the Lord was going to return*, and is *only just now teaching them for the very first time about the details of his return?* In fact, how could the Thessalonians know about a doctrine completely unknown in the history of the church until the infamous vision of Margaret MacDonald in the year 1830?

A lot of light can be shed on this topic by clearing up the mystery around Paul's use of the word *harpazo*. Paul used the verb for a very specific reason. In the culture of the Roman Empire, the word referred to a person's being "snatched away" in death. Fate or Fortune, understood as gods, are frequently pictured in both Greek and Latin literature as "snatching" loved ones away to Hades or the underworld. Death, so to speak, had "raptured" them. The word often appeared as a sad and hopeless inscription on tombstones: "snatched away" — "raptured". In light of the good news of the Gospel, Paul turns the word around.

Believers are not snatched away by death, but caught up into life. He is not using the word to refer to a secret return of Christ in which believers are removed from the world. He is simply contrasting the pagan belief in fate *snatching people away to Hades* with the Christian belief that Christ *snatches them up into eternal life*. Believers are caught up, he continues, to meet the Lord in the clouds. This image is associated with both the ascension of Christ (Ac. 1: 9) and his return (Mt. 24:30; Mk. 13:36; Rev. 1:7). It is rooted in Daniel's vision of the Son of man coming with the clouds of heaven (Dn. 7:13). The clouds are not an indicator of geographical location! *They are a consistent Biblical sign of the presence of God*. Remember the pillar of cloud which led and guarded the Israelites, or the cloud of glory that hovered over the tabernacle and later filled the temple? When he returns, his presence will fill the entire cosmos. No one in their right mind should believe that Christ is descending like a modern airplane to meet believers at, let's say, 10,000 feet, whereupon the plane resumes its ascent. But Christ, who ascended into the realm of eternity, is now descending back into this world, just as the angels promised the watching disciples he would (Ac. 1:11, where a cloud accompanies him). As he left this world, now he is returning to reclaim it. He has no intention of leaving again.

A "meeting" with the Lord

Paul's next phase is extremely significant. The purpose of the believers being caught up is to meet the Lord. The Greek text says literally that believers will be caught up "for a meeting with the Lord" (verse 17). "Meeting" is the Greek word *apantesis*. And by examining its use in Greek literature, we find this word is very similar in meaning to *parousia*. A *parousia* was the term for the "coming" of a king or high official to a city, whereupon the citizens went out to meet him and escort him back into the city. An *apantesis* was the term for a formal reception given for the dignitary at his *parousia*. The civic leaders would go outside the city to meet the important personage, shower him with shouts of praise, and then escort him back into the city. The *parousia* is the coming of the king, and the *apantesis* is the reception given when he arrives. The key to understanding both is that the king is escorted by the citizens *back into the city* where his kingship is affirmed and honored. This is completely opposite to the idea of Darby's rapture, in which believers go outside the city *in order to be taken out of the world entirely*, while the world is handed over to a devastating tribulation in which God has lost control and Satan is running rampant.

The Thessalonians would have understood immediately what both of these words meant. The word *apantesis* was so common it was used as a loan word in Latin, where Cicero writes of the *apantesis* Julius Caesar was receiving from the Roman towns as he returned from his military triumphs abroad. As Caesar approached the various cities, the citizens went out to meet him, then escorted him back into the city where he was honored. Even more remarkably, the word was known by the Rabbis and used as a loan word in Hebrew, where the leading citizens were described as going out of the city for an *apantesis* with the ruler, then escorting him back into the city for him to take up his rule.

Now let's look at the two other places in the New Testament where the word appears. In both these cases, the meaning of the word *is spelled out plainly in the text itself.* When the Christians in Rome learned that Paul was approaching the city, they sent a delegation quite a distance out of the city, to a place called The Three Taverns (*Tres tabernae* in Latin), for an *apantesis* in his honor. What happened next? *They escorted him all the way back into Rome* (Ac. 28:15-16). In the parable of the ten virgins which, very significantly, is about the Lord's return, the young women "go out" for an *apantesis* with the approaching bridegroom. After the *apantesis*, the wise virgins *then accompany him back into the wedding feast* (Mt. 25:6-10), which of course is the wedding feast of the Lamb (Rev. 19:9), which is pictured as taking place *immediately after* the return of Christ. *These verses prove beyond doubt that Paul was not teaching a rapture.* He was painting a picture of Christians going out to meet Jesus as he descends in the presence of God (the "clouds") in order to escort him back into the new eternal city and proclaim his rule over it. *This passage also teaches that there is no thousand year gap between the descending of the Lord in the clouds and the inauguration of the new Jerusalem.* Jesus was speaking of his final return, not of an earthly millennial rule, for in the passage from Matthew quoted above he tells the disciples what will happen immediately after the *apantesis:* "When the Son of Man comes in his glory, and all the angels with him, then he will sit on his glorious throne. Before him will be gathered all the nations, and he will separate people one from another… and these (the wicked) will go away into eternal punishment, but the righteous into eternal life" (Mt. 25:31-32, 46). There is only one return of Christ, and it is followed immediately by the king sitting on his throne to exercise his rule, the event described in Rev. 20:11-15 as the Great White Throne judgment.

Who then is left behind? An insight from the Gospels

One more passage remains to be commented on. Discussing the events surrounding his return, Jesus teaches his disciples that no one will know its day or hour (Mt. 24:36). Darby's followers, as all of us know, have been notorious for generations for violating Jesus' words and predicting dates which never come to pass — and then never repenting or apologizing because they got it wrong. Jesus continues his teaching by by saying this, "For as were the days of Noah, so will be the coming of the Son of Man. For as in those days before the flood they were eating and drinking, marrying and giving in marriage, until the day when Noah entered the ark, and they were unaware until the flood came and swept them all away, so will be the coming of the Son of Man. Then two men will be in the field; one will be taken and one left. Two women will be grinding at the mill; one will be taken and one left" (Mt 24:38-41). Here we have the origin of the famous phrase "left behind." But what exactly does the passage teach? The key phrase is given at the beginning: *"For as were the days of Noah."* It is without doubt the wicked who were swept away in the flood, as Jesus himself states explicitly in verse 39. *Noah and his family* were the ones left behind who survived the deluge. Now, in like manner, Jesus tells us in verses 40-41, the wicked will be taken away at his return, and the saved will be left behind. And Matthew also makes it clear that the return Jesus is speaking of, *when this division of taken away and left behind occurs*, far from being a secret rapture, will be visible not only to the saved but to the entire cosmos, "As the lightning comes from the east and shines as far as the west, so will be the coming [*parousia*] of the Son of Man" (Mt. 24:27). This is the same entirely visible *parousia* Paul teaches the Thessalonians about, where the saints are caught up to meet the Lord as he returns, the one and only coming of Jesus which will sweep away the wicked *while the righteous are left behind.*

It is little wonder that the authors of the Left Behind books had to write them in the form of novels, for that is what they are — pure fiction.

CHAPTER FOUR

THE LAST DAYS

People often speak in fearful terms of what is going to happen in the "last days." When they use this phrase, of course, they are referring to the events immediately preceding the return of Christ. Dispensationalism has taught us that God will lose control of his creation. Conditions will become so dire that he will mercifully airlift the entire church out before the very worst events take place in a seven year period called the tribulation. In spite of the hope offered by this exit strategy, an enormous amount of fear remains because of the expectation that Satan is moving fast to establish world domination, and no one is sure how much Christians will suffer even before the rapture.

We've already seen reason to question the entire worldview

dispensationalism offers us. *But what if we don't even understand the concept of the last days correctly?* At the beginning of Revelation, John makes several significant references to the account in Daniel 2 of Nebuchadnezzar's dream of a statue with four parts made of different metals. Using the Aramaic language, Daniel speaks of things God has "shown" him which will take place in a time described as the "latter days" or "after this/after these things" (Dn. 2:28-29, 45). God subsequently reveals to Daniel that these prophecies are to be sealed up until "the time of the end" (Dn. 12:9).

In Rev. 1:1, 19, using the Greek translation of the Old Testament, John quotes Daniel's words. He says that God has likewise "shown" him what is to take place, just as he "showed" Daniel. But there is a significant alteration. According to Daniel, God "made known" to Nebuchadnezzar "what will be in the latter days" (Dn. 2:28). But God "made known" to John the things that must take place "speedily" or "imminently" (the Greek word is *tachus*). The things Daniel foresaw would not take place until the time of the end, but the whole range of events revealed to John in the various visions of Revelation *are about to happen or have even begun to happen*. The force of the phrase "the things that must soon take place" (Rev. 1:1) is similar to Jesus' declaration, "the kingdom of God is at hand" (Mk. 1:15). The events are right here, even now beginning to happen. John deliberately uses the words of Daniel to emphasize the fact that *Daniel's future is now present,* and that *the events prophesied long age are now commencing.*

Daniel spoke of momentous events in the distant future. In the latter days, the fourth earthly kingdom of his vision would be shattered by the rock of the kingdom of God (Dn. 2:44). The coming of this kingdom is connected with the appearance of the "son of man" who will rule over it (Dn. 7:13-14). In the vision of Revelation 4 and 5, John alludes clearly to the Daniel text and sees these prophesied events as fulfilled in the death and resurrection of Jesus Christ. He is the Son of man prophesied in Daniel 7, and he has been exalted to the right hand of God to receive an eternal kingdom. Jesus himself interprets Daniel's earth-shattering rock as fulfilled in his own ministry, "Everyone who falls on that stone will be broken to pieces, and when it falls on anyone, it will crush him" (Lk. 20:18). The latter days to Daniel were a future far off and whose secrets were to be sealed until the end time (Dn. 12:9). To John, however, the secrets have been unsealed (Rev. 5:5), and the events foretold by the prophet are now unfolding before his own eyes.

The events prophesied by Daniel have thus begun to occur, set in motion by the death and resurrection of Jesus Christ. All that is about to happen — from the events occurring in the seven churches of Asia to the events which will occur as the rest of the church age unfolds — are now being unsealed or revealed, which is what Revelation is all about. The "latter days" or "time of the end" is at hand, and its events are beginning to happen, in the same sense that Jesus announced the arrival of the kingdom of God at the outset of his ministry. The events of the end are no longer for a distant future, but are right in front of us. The visions John unfolds as Revelation progresses represent events which are occurring in the life of the seven churches to whom he was writing, and will continue until Jesus returns. They are indeed the events of the "last days" in the sense in which the New Testament as a whole uses this term.

But this is not the "last days" portrayed by dispensationalist teaching, which defines the term as referring only to events immediately preceding the return of Christ. It turns out that we have been waiting for something that began two thousand years ago! *The last days are now.* If this seems a strange thought, consider this. Peter declared that at Pentecost the "last days" prophesied by Joel *had begun.* What was happening on the day of Pentecost, Peter informed the crowd, was exactly what Joel had prophesied centuries before, "And in the *last days* it shall be, God declares, that I will pour out my Spirit on all flesh" (Ac. 2:17). He then moves immediately and seamlessly in interpreting Joel as announcing both Pentecost (verses 17-19), and (without noting any time delay) the prophesied day of the Lord (the last judgment) in verses 19-21. Thus he collapses all of history after Christ into the category of the last days, and declares we are living in them now.

A similar understanding is found in Hebrews, "In these *last days* he has spoken to us by his Son" (Heb. 1:2). It is also found in James, "You have laid up treasure in the *last days*" (Jas. 5:3). And it is found in Peter's writings, "[He] was made manifest in the *last times*" (1 Pet.1:20). John elsewhere interprets it this way himself, "Children, it is the *last hour*" (1 Jn. 2:18). The Bible understands the last days to be the days commencing with the death and resurrection of Christ, and concluding with his return. This time period — otherwise known as the church age — is the age in which John lived and the age in which we still live, and it is this age which is described in the visions of Revelation, in the historical record of Acts and in the various letters of the New Testament.

For John and for each one of us, the last days are thus a present reality. God gave the visions of Revelation to John so that he would be able to understand what was happening around him and respond rightly, so that saints of the tenth century could understand, so that you and I can understand, and so that saints of the future can understand. Grasping the truth that the last days are now is an indispensable basis for understanding the events recorded in the book of Revelation, which is a record of the history between Christ's resurrection and his return.

It is clear that throughout history, God has asserted his right to be sovereign ruler of the cosmos. His authority is contested by the enemy, and we live on a spiritual battleground. Biblical scholars have likened this to the events of World War II. D-day in June 1944 was the point at which everyone knew the ultimate outcome. Yet it was ten months, many battles and thousands of lives later before V-day took place. The church lives between these two markers. The kingdom is here, yet not in its final form. Christ's resurrection is D-day and his return is V-day. In these last days of history, between these two great events, we fight a battle with many casualties and much cost, yet it is a battle we are destined to win. The church has always acknowledged that Christ is Lord over history. Revelation itself describes Christ as the "ruler of the kings on earth" (1:5), the One who has "glory and dominion for ever and ever." Both God and Christ are referred to as the "Alpha and the Omega," (Rev. 1:8; 22:13), the Lord of the beginning of history, the end of history and everything in between. The last days began with the eruption of the kingdom of God into human history, the rock that will crush the kingdoms of this earth (Dan. 2:44-45; Lk. 20:18). It is not the time of God's retreat, but of his victory.

However we interpret the passages in the New Testament, including Revelation, which describe the events immediately prior to the Lord's return, we should be aware that they are only the *last events of the last days*, days we have been living in for two thousand years, days of the reign and rule of God as he prepares his world for the triumphant return of the King.

CHAPTER FIVE

THE SIGN OF THE LORD'S COMING

The disciples asked Jesus the question burning in their hearts, "What will be the sign of your coming and of the end of the age?" (Mt. 24:3). Jesus unfolded a long list of events that would take place, including wars, famines and earthquakes, culminating in two apparently opposing trends. On the one hand, there would be lawlessness, betrayals and deception, and on the other hand, "this gospel of the kingdom will be proclaimed throughout the whole world as a testimony to all nations, and then the end will come" (Mt. 24:14). Mark records Jesus' words in a similar way, "The gospel must first be proclaimed to all nations" (Mk. 13:10). The word "nations" is the Greek word *ethne*, representing what we would call people groups, rather than political entities. While it might be said that the gospel has come to virtually every political state on earth, it cannot be said that it has come to every people group. There are approximately two hundred nations in the world, but there are thousands of people groups.

Jesus' clear statement to the disciples thus constitutes a big red flag in relation to predictions of his imminent return. While we cannot say with absolute certainty that every people group has *not* been reached in the way Jesus spoke of, it seems highly unlikely in light of all we know about the extent of world missions. The Bible does not even exist in hundreds of languages, and every missions organization will tell you there are numerous totally unreached people groups. Instead of taking Jesus' statement as a sign of his imminent return, it seems better to take it as an exhortation to fulfill the Great Commission in the way Jesus surely wanted it to be fulfilled: that every people group on earth would have the opportunity of understanding what the message of the gospel truly is. As Oswald J. Smith said a century ago, why should we prioritize preaching to those who have already been presented with the Gospel when there are uncounted multitudes who have never yet once heard it?

But why, apart from God's care for all nations, is it so important that the gospel go to every people group? The unfolding story line of the Bible shows us why: Jesus must succeed where all who went before him failed. To explain what I mean by this, we have to go back to the beginning of history.

The commission to Adam

Eden was the first temple — a temple being constituted by the presence of God — and Adam was the first priest. His duties were to serve God in the garden and to guard it from evil. This is confirmed by the interesting fact that the same words which described Adam's duties in the garden — to "work/serve" and to "keep/guard" (Gen. 2:15) — are used to describe the primary duties of the priests in the tabernacle. The duty of the priests and Levites was to "serve" in the tabernacle and to "guard" against anything unclean entering it (Num. 3:5-10). Adam's duty was also to serve and guard — to serve God in the temple of the garden and to guard against anything unclean entering it. Just like Aaron and his sons in the tabernacle, Adam was a priest in the temple of the Garden where the presence of God dwelt.

But in Gen. 1:28, God had given Adam and Eve a further commission, "And God said to them, 'Be fruitful and multiply and fill the whole earth and subdue it.'" The means by which this goal was to be accomplished is stated in verse 27, "So God created man in his own image, in the image of God he created him; male and female he created them." Because they were created in his image, they were able to reflect and to enforce his rule over the whole earth. In other words, Adam and Eve were to function as God's vice-rulers or vice-regents on earth. Not only were they to serve and guard within the garden, they were to *extend the boundaries of the garden outward* into the inhospitable lands outside — the lands into which they were eventually expelled. God's goal was that the whole creation would be rendered habitable for Adam and his descendants. This is confirmed by Isa. 45:18, "For thus says the Lord, who created the heavens (he is God!), who formed the earth and made it (he established it; he did not create it empty, he formed it to be inhabited!)." The ultimate goal of God was that, through the earth being subdued and made habitable, he himself would be glorified throughout his creation. The realm of God's rule, which was initially limited to the garden temple of Eden, was to be extended throughout the whole world by his image-bearers. The fact that Adam and Eve were to become "one flesh" (Gen. 2:24) further emphasizes the fact that their function as male and female involved beginning to fill the earth with people as the garden temple was extended. Though it cannot be proven from the text of Genesis, there is no reason to believe that they did not have a significant number of offspring before the fall, even though Genesis records by name only those born after it.

The reason we have not entertained this possibility is surely because we have associated sexual activity with fallen human nature, even though it is far more likely that sex, like everything else, existed in perfect harmony with our relationship with God, and was first marred by the consequences of our sin. If Adam and Eve were thus co-operating with God in the commission to extend his kingdom prior to the fall, this in turn would answer the question of where the other human beings referred to in the immediate post-fall history of Genesis 4 came from.

The commission to Israel

As the Bible makes clear, Adam failed in his task. He did not guard the garden temple, but instead permitted the entrance of the evil serpent who brought sin and rebellion into the very place of God's presence. Instead of extending the divine presence outward, Adam and Eve were cut off from that presence. The kingdom mandate apparently lay in ruins. But God, in his great mercy, had not given up on his creation, for Adam's commission was in fact passed on to others. This explains why in Gen. 9:1,7, God commanded Noah after the flood to be fruitful and multiply, and to fill the earth. It explains why in Gen. 17:2, 6 and 8, God promised Abraham that he would multiply his descendants and make him fruitful, and why in Gen. 22:17-18 he said that in Abraham's seed all the nations of the earth would be blessed. It explains why in Gen. 26:4, God told Isaac he would multiply his descendants and that all the nations of the earth would be blessed by them. It explains why in Gen. 35:11-12, God told Jacob to be fruitful and multiply, and that a company of nations would come from him. And it explains why in Gen. 47:27, it is recorded of Israel that they lived in Egypt and were fruitful and became very numerous.

The elements of the commission to Adam (to be fruitful and

multiply and to fill the earth) are repeated over and over again from Noah through Abraham, Isaac and Jacob, and on to Israel as a nation (Gen. 47:27; Exod. 1:7). It is why, on the eve of their entry into the promised land, God told Israel he would bless them, multiply them, make them fruitful and enable them to fill the earth by subduing the nations around them (Deut. 7:13-16). And notice another interesting phenomenon. Every time, from Noah to Jacob, that God spoke these words of command and promise, renewing the commission to Adam, these men responded by (1) pitching a tabernacle (2) on a mountain, (3) building an altar, (4) worshipping God, and (5) almost always calling the place the house of God. The combination of these five elements occurs elsewhere in the Old Testament only in the building of the tabernacle of Moses and the temple of Solomon. What is happening? The patriarchs are building worship areas *in fulfillment of the original commission* of Gen. 1:26-28 that their offspring are to spread out to subdue the world from the base of a divine sanctuary or temple, no matter how small that temple may be in its beginnings. These informal temples pointed to the later tabernacle and the temple from which Israel as a nation was to fulfill the commission by branching out over all the earth. So God not only graciously renewed the commission, in the process he began all over again to create a place, no matter how restricted, for his dwelling on earth. God had provided a base of operations from which the kingdom mandate could be fulfilled.

Yet Israel, like Adam and Noah before them, failed. Solomon was the first king to extend his rule to the full extent of the original boundaries God had promised Israel through Abraham (Gen. 22:18), yet no sooner had the temple been built than Solomon fell into sin and disobedience, and within a generation his kingdom was reduced to a remnant of its size and power. Eventually, Israel and Judah both went into exile and even when some exiles came back, they were never able to regain rule over their land. And when the promised Messiah at last came, they rejected him. Yet still there remained a prophetic shred of hope, present in the words of Isaiah spoken to a failing nation, "It is too light a thing that you should be my servant to raise up the tribes of Jacob and to bring back the preserved of Israel; I will make you as a light for the nations, that my salvation may reach to the end of the earth" (Isa. 49:6). Israel had failed, but God's plan had not. This passage is a stunning reminder of the fact that all Old Testament prophecies are fulfilled in Christ, who is himself the true Israel, the seed of Abraham and the son of David. Through this one Son of man, the true Israel, God's kingdom mandate will be fulfilled and his salvation will reach to the ends of the earth.

The commission fulfilled in Jesus

Matthew's Gospel begins with the Greek expression *biblos geneseos*, literally, the "book of the beginning" or the "book of genesis". The only other places in the Greek Bible this phrase occurs are in Gen. 2:4, which reads literally, "This is the book of the genesis of the heavens and the earth," and Gen. 5:1, which reads literally, "This is the book of the genesis of Adam." Matthew borrows the phrase from the Old Testament text to make two things clear: that he is narrating the record of a new genesis, a new creation in Christ, and that Jesus is the second Adam, who will succeed where the first Adam failed.

And Jesus will also succeed where Israel failed. Whereas Israel spent forty years in the wilderness succumbing to the devil, Jesus spent forty days in the wilderness overcoming him, accomplishing the defeat of the devil that should have occurred in the garden. After his defeat of Satan, Jesus appointed twelve apostles who, representing the church, constitute the government of God in the new creation, even as the twelve tribes of Israel did in the old creation. His healings and miracles represent the beginning of the restoration of Adam's creation from its fallen state, and also the fulfillment of what Isaiah prophesied would happen when Israel experienced her end-time restoration to God, "Then shall the eyes of the blind be opened, and the ears of the deaf unstopped; then shall the lame man leap like a deer, and the tongue of the mute sing for joy" (Isa. 35:5-6). The restoration of Israel commences not in a mid-twentieth century political event, but in the ministry of Jesus and the arrival of the kingdom, and moves forward not through a modern political state but through God's chosen race, royal priesthood and holy nation (1 Pet. 2:9), his people of the new covenant, both

Jew and Gentile, whom Paul calls the "Israel of God" (Gal. 6:16). Throughout all this, Israel never ceases to exist, but its conditions of entry are changed and its boundaries widened to include people from all nations.

Adam was given stewardship over the whole earth (Gen. 1:28). He was commissioned to extend the garden to the ends of the earth. What Adam failed to do, Israel under the old covenant also failed to do. As a nation, Israel was also charged with bringing the knowledge of God to the nations of the earth. This was the essence of the promise given to Abraham that in him "all the families of the earth" would be blessed (Gen. 12:3). But where Adam and Israel both failed, Christ will succeed. Through his atoning sacrifice, the gospel has gone to the nations of the world, and the saints of all ages are able to enter the eternal city. The promise given to Abraham that in his seed all the families of the earth would be blessed is fulfilled through Christ (Gal. 3:16). *That is why he will not return until the commission is complete.* The "great commission" to disciple the nations (Mt. 28:18-20) is nothing more nor less than the fulfillment of the original commission given to Adam to be fruitful and multiply. Jesus will not return until the commission is fulfilled and every people group on earth has been reached with the Gospel.

Jesus warned us not to get led astray by wars, rumors of wars and unusual natural events, yet these are the very things, from numerous conflicts in the middle east and elsewhere to blood red moons, that dispensational writers and preachers have used to predict the Lord's return, never repenting, apologizing or returning their massive book and movie royalties when their predictions are proven false.

None of us know the day nor the hour. Jesus said not even the Son of man knew! How presumptuous to believe that we know what he does not.

All we do know is what he has told us. He will not return until his mission is complete.

CHAPTER SIX

THE TWO WITNESSES

Many years ago an individual I knew, a man of both educational and professional success, fell into a serious deception. That became apparent when he confided in me that he was one of the two witnesses of Revelation 11. The depth of the enemy's hold over him was later revealed. He had fallen into such a severe moral failure that legal charges were brought against him, and in due course he lost everything. It is impossible to separate our personal walk with Christ and our intellectual understanding of Scripture. Could his delusional self-identification have led to the belief he could justifiably take advantage of other people? A warp in our walk will often lead to a warp in our theology.

That individual, of course, was an adherent of dispensational theology, which claims that only a literal interpretation of Revelation is acceptable (though I am *not* saying that his dispensational views caused his moral failure). That means Revelation 11 must be speaking of two literal individuals arising as prophets. But is this in fact the case? It turns out it is not, and the solution to the correct interpretation is found in the multiple allusions in the text to the Old Testament.

These witnesses are not individuals, but are to be identified with the church as it bears witness from the days John first wrote until the day of the Lord's return.

This interpretation is based on a number of considerations:

(1) They are called "lampstands" (11:4), which Rev. 1:12-25 clearly identifies as the churches.
(2) They are also called olive trees (verse 4). Lampstands filled with olive oil also allude to the Holy Spirit, who is poured out upon all God's people (not just two), who will then prophesy (Joel 2:28-32; Ac. 2:17-21), which is the very function of the witnesses (11:6).
(3) The words that Christ speaks to John here, "the beast.... will make war on them and conquer them and kill them" (Rev. 11:7), are the same as the angel spoke to Daniel. Daniel was told that the horn that arises from the fourth beast "made war with the saints and prevailed over them" (Dn. 7:21). The parallel shows that the two witnesses are symbolic representatives *of the people of God as a whole*, for

it is the people of God who are referred to in the Daniel text, *not certain individuals*. The same event is described again in Rev. 20:8-10, where the beast makes final war against "the camp of the saints and the beloved city."

(4) According to 11:9-13, the whole world will witness the (apparent) defeat of the witnesses. This is only understandable as a portrayal of something happening to the worldwide church.

(5) The witnesses prophesy for three and a half years, the same time that the holy city (clearly the church) is trampled underfoot (11:2), the same time the "woman" of 12:6 (also clearly representing the church) is oppressed, and the same time those dwelling in heaven (all the deceased saints awaiting the resurrection of 13:6) are blasphemed.

The fact that there are two witnesses is significant. The words for "witness" (verse 3) and "testimony" (verse 7) are legal terms in Greek. The presence of two witnesses was the Old Testament requirement for determining a legal offense (Num. 35:30; Deut. 17:16). That is why Jesus sent out disciples in groups of two as legal witnesses to the gospel message (Matt. 18:16; Lk. 10:1-24; Jn. 8:17). Paul followed the same procedure (2 Cor. 13:1; 1 Tim. 5:19). Two angels, not one or three, bore witness to the resurrection (Lk. 24:3) and to the certainty of Christ's return (Ac. 1:10-11).

In verse 6, the witnesses are revealed as the fulfillment of the Old Testament expectation that Moses and Elijah would return in the latter days to restore Israel, "They have the power to shut the sky, that no rain may fall during the days of their prophesying, and they have power over the waters to turn them into blood and to strike the earth with every kind of plague, as often as they desire." In Mk. 9:4-7 Moses and Elijah, as the two witnesses legally needed, appear on the mountain in order to testify that Jesus is the Son of God. Moses and Elijah represent the law and the prophets, and the comparison to them here indicates that the church is the fulfillment of the latter-days restoration of Israel prophesied throughout the Old Testament.

The specific references in verse 6 are to Elijah's power to withhold rain from the earth (1 Kings 11) and Moses' ability to turn water into blood (Exod. 7:17-25). Use of the word "plague" also takes us back to the ministry of Moses. The three and a half year period of the witnesses' ministry corresponds to the same time period of Elijah's ministry of judgment by drought (Lk. 4:25; Jas. 5:17), and to the forty-two encampments of Israel under Moses in the desert. The judgments are not literal, but are symbolic of all judgments God brings against unbelievers to remind them of their rebellion and their eventual doom. The judgments symbolized by the fire and blood speak of any means by which God reminds unbelievers of his authority over creation. Fire is frequently connected with judgment in the Bible —think of Sodom, of God's judgments on Mt. Sinai, or of Elijah calling down fire on the soldiers sent to arrest him.

Particularly significant for the understanding of this passage is the incident in which the disciples suggest to Jesus that they follow Elijah's example by calling down fire on the disobedient villages of the Samaritans (Lk. 9:51-56). Jesus rejected their request, but shortly afterward sent out thirty-six groups of two (legal) witnesses to declare both the grace and the judgment of God. In the same way, the two witnesses in John's vision declare the judgment of God not by calling down literal fire, but by declaring the Gospel and the consequences of disobeying it.

The description of the witnesses occurs in the midst of the vision of the trumpet plagues, and this is no accident. The nature of the plagues the witnesses bring are closely related to the trumpet plagues, which in turn are rooted in the plagues of Exodus. In both cases, the judgments are described as "plagues" (verse 6 and 9:20). They are directed against "those who dwell on the earth" (8:13 and 11:10). They are initiated by those who are given power to pronounce God's judgment (9:13 and 11:6). Both involve famine (8:7 and 11:6), death (9:15 and 11:5) and harm of various kinds (9:10 and 11:5). Fire comes from the mouths of those with the power to kill (9:17-18 and 11:5). Water turns into blood (8:8 and 11:6). There are supernatural phenomena involving the sky or heavens (8:10 and 11:6). Finally, the result of all this is that unbelievers are "tormented" (9:5-6 and 11:10). Both sections conclude with some unbelievers being killed (9:20 and 11:13). This is not surprising, because all four sets of seven judgments in Revelation describe events from Christ's resurrection until his return. The description of the witness of the church in chapter 11, therefore, is another way of telling the same story.

If my acquaintance of many years ago had only understood this chapter correctly, it just might have saved him from starting down a road that led to his destruction.

CHAPTER SEVEN

THE APOSTASY AND THE RISE OF THE ANTICHRIST

Paul's instructions in his first letter to the Thessalonians failed to satisfy all their questions, so in his second letter he returns to the topic of the return of Christ. As our comments in chapter five made clear, the Lord *could return* at any time after the kingdom has reached every people group on earth. However, certain events will also take place which will signify that the time of return is approaching, even if we cannot put a date on it. These events are so significant and clear in their dimensions that no one will have to write books speculating about them!

The first event that must take place is the apostasy or rebellion, "Let no one deceive you in any way. For that day will not come, unless the rebellion (*apostasia*) comes first" (2 Thess.

2:3a). Paul uses the definite article before the word, which has the effect of making it *the* apostasy — "the apostasy that you surely know about." The reason they know about it is because he has taught them about it, "Do you not remember that when I was still with you I told you these things?" (verse 5). Although the Thessalonians knew what he was referring to, what he said to them is (sadly but providentially) not entirely clear to us.

In Greek literature, the word "apostasy" referred to a political or military rebellion, but in the Greek translation of the Old Testament it takes on a religious significance — apostasy is a rebellion against God. When we look at the New Testament, we find a consistent message that the last days before the return of Christ will be characterized by an increase in rebellion and wickedness of various sorts (Mt. 24:11-24; Mk. 13:3-23; 1 Tim. 4:1-2; 2 Tim. 3:1-9; 2 Pet. 3:3-4; Jude 17-18). Consider also the vision in Rev. 11:7-13 of the two witnesses (who corporately represent the church) being subject to apparent death and destruction in the very last period of history, before being miraculously resurrected as Christ returns. The same idea is represented here by the "apostasy." It is a massive rebellion against God in the final days before the day of the Lord arrives. The passage in Revelation 11 suggests that the rebellion is not primarily a falling away of believers as much as an increase in wickedness by unbelievers, who in various places in Revelation are pictured as gathering together to attack the church (13:7; 16:14-16; 19:19; 20:7-10).

Yet the rebellion also includes a falling away in the church; commitment wavers as persecution intensifies. Jesus seems to be referring to people who are at least professing to be believers when he says that "many will fall away and betray one another and hate one another. And many false prophets will arise and lead many astray. And because lawlessness will be increased, the love of many will grow cold. But the one who endures to the end will be saved (Mt. 24:10-13a). The letters of the New Testament assume, of course, that there are professing but not true believers in every church — some examples, particularly the immoral practitioners in Corinth, the false teachers in Galatia and the heretics in Colossae are obvious. Jude warns explicitly that ungodly people have infiltrated the church in order to destroy it, and false prophets have invaded the churches in Pergamum and Thyatira. The warnings in Hebrews against walking away from the faith assume that some in the church are not truly saved. The strategy of Satan in every age has been to send his agents into the church to corrupt it, and in the events near the return of Christ this tactic will only increase.

This apostasy or rebellion sets the stage for the revealing of the one Paul calls the "man of lawlessness." He says this, "… and the man of lawlessness is revealed, the son of destruction, who opposes and exalts himself against every so-called god or object of worship, so that he takes his seat in the temple of God, proclaiming himself to be God" (2 Thess. 2:3b-4). The phrase "the son of destruction" refers not so much to the fact that he brings destruction (though he certainly does) as to the fact that *he will go to destruction.* The word "destruction" (*apoleia*) in the New Testament generally refers to the eternal destruction of the lost. Paul is borrowing a theme from Daniel's prophecy of a coming king who will profane the temple and set up in it "the abomination that makes desolate" (Dn. 11:31). He will exalt himself above every god and "speak astonishing things against the God of gods" (Dn. 11:36). Paul adds to his comments the statement that "the mystery of lawlessness is already at work" (verse 7), yet is at present restrained.

The Jews considered that Daniel's prophecy was fulfilled when the wicked Syrian king Antiochus Epiphanes desecrated the temple in 167 BC, yet they saw further fulfillments in actual or attempted desecrations by the Roman general Pompey in 63 BC and the Emperor Caligula in AD 40. Paul is thus using a well-established Jewish theme of a wicked ruler who will desecrate the temple by setting himself up as a god. But he is also drawing on the teachings of Jesus. Jesus spoke clearly, as we saw above, of a "falling away" in the days before he returned (Mt. 24:10). False prophets would arise to corrupt God's people (verse 11). There would be an increase of "lawlessness" (verse 13). Jesus himself is mining Daniel's prophecies, for he goes on to quote Daniel in verse 15 regarding the "abomination of desolation," but as a prophetic word speaking of events surrounding the siege of Jerusalem in AD 66-70, when the temple was destroyed. When in AD

68 the Jewish sect called the Zealots desecrated the temple, the Christian community took it as the fulfillment of Jesus' prophetic warning and did what Jesus had told them to do — they fled the city, and were thus saved from the holocaust that took place when the Romans destroyed the city and its people two years later. So it seems that there were multiple initial fulfillments of the temple's desecration, all pointing to a final manifestation of evil in the very last days before the day of the Lord.

It is very difficult to escape the conclusion that Paul was pointing to a specific individual who will be the very incarnation of evil. Paul uses the word *parousia* in reference to both Christ's return (verse 8) and the appearing of the antichrist (verse 9), which is the only time in the New Testament the word *parousia* is used of anyone other than Christ. The implication is clear: this individual is a personal demonic counterfeit of Christ. The climax of his self-exaltation is that he "takes his seat in the temple of God, proclaiming himself to be God" (2 Thess. 2:4).

But what is the temple he is referring to? Scholars are divided between reference to a literal temple and reference to a spiritual temple (which would then be the church). In favor of the latter is the fact that, outside of this verse, all seven uses of the word "temple" by Paul in his letters clearly refer to the church or individual believers. Paul would surely have taught the Thessalonians, just as he did the Corinthians, that they were the true temple of God. In this case, the apostasy would occur in the church and the man of lawlessness would proclaim himself as the church's head.

Paul uses the definite article here in the phrase "the temple of God," meaning *the* temple which you Thessalonians know about, which suggests a reference to the Jerusalem temple. The soon to take place destruction of the temple in Jerusalem points to a latter-days destruction of God's spiritual temple, the church. The Roman emperor Caligula had tried to install himself as a god in the Jerusalem temple only a few years prior to Paul's writing the letter, and was stopped only by the fact he was assassinated before he could do it. With this event fresh in mind, Paul may be using the common Jewish theme of pagan rulers desecrating the temple and declaring themselves gods in it to illustrate figuratively a future event in which an eschatological antichrist figure will attempt to take the place of God.

The Jerusalem temple, of course, was destroyed about or very shortly after the probable time of Paul's own death, and Paul would have been well aware that Jesus had prophesied its destruction within one generation (Mt. 24:1- 2, 34). It is therefore highly unlikely that Paul expected this figure to seat himself in the literal Jerusalem temple. When the Jewish Zealots desecrated the temple in AD 68, as noted above, it caused the departure of the Christian community *en masse* from Jerusalem, as they recognized it as the fulfillment of

Jesus' warning to flee when it happened (Mt. 24:15-16). Yet this did not precipitate any of these eschatological events or the Lord's return.

We conclude, therefore, that Paul is predicting a time, shortly before the Lord's return, when after a massive rebellion against God, a satanically-inspired individual commits a worldwide desecration by proclaiming himself to be God in a manner no one else had ever attempted, and almost certainly attempting to claim or force the church's allegiance at the same time. The rebellion, of course, does not occur only in the church. Both Jesus and Paul are talking about something even more widespread when they refer to the falling away, that is, a general rebellion of humanity against God, which also coheres with the consistent teaching of Revelation.

One very legitimate question arises. Why is this figure commonly often called the antichrist, when Paul never uses the word? The terminology comes from 1 and 2 John. John reminds his readers twice that they have been told that the antichrist is coming (1 Jn. 2:18; 4:4), yet now "many antichrists have come" (1 Jn. 2:18b; 2 Jn. 1:7). The antichrist is said by John to deny the Father and the Son. He goes on to talk about false prophets who have "the spirit of the antichrist, which you heard was coming and now is in the world already" (1 Jn. 4:3). Note here a parallel between John and Paul. According to John, the spirit of antichrist is already present (working to undermine the first century churches), but is also manifest in an apparently personal form (false teachers who deny Christ). Paul teaches that the "mystery of lawlessness is already at work" (at the time Paul was writing), but "the lawless one will be revealed" later (2 Thess. 2:6, 8). That is, the lawless or ungodly spirit will manifest itself in a person who attempts to take the place of Christ himself (anti-Christ), even working false signs and wonders (2 Thess. 2:9), just like the magicians of Egypt who opposed God. The parallelism between John and Paul points to the emergence of a final incarnation of evil, which could legitimately be termed the "man of lawlessness," the "son of destruction," or the "antichrist." We will say more about this man of evil in chapter nine.

That evil, however, is presently restrained, the subject Paul addresses next.

CHAPTER EIGHT

THE RESTRAINER AND THE BINDING OF SATAN

Paul's discussion in 2 Thessalonians 2 of the rebellion and the rise of the antichrist now leads him into another topic. He turns to the subject of the binding of Satan and the work of a mysterious figure called the restrainer, "And you know what is restraining him now so that he may be revealed in his time. For the mystery of lawlessness is already at work. Only he who now restrains it will do so until he is out of the way" (verses 6-7). The purpose clause ("so that he may be revealed") refers to the hand of God, who is in control of the whole train of events as he works out his purposes. The mystery of lawlessness is already at work, but it is held in check by one who, under the hand of God, restrains the rise of the antichrist figure.

The word "mystery" in Paul's writings always refers to a divine purpose. The gospel itself is referred to as a mystery which has been hidden, but at an appropriate moment is revealed by God (Rom. 16:25; Eph. 3:6; Col. 1:26). The mystery referred to here is presently hidden from plain sight, but behind the scenes it is very much at work. The fact that "mystery" is linked with the plan of God alerts us to a complex situation where even the works of the enemy (such as Paul's thorn in the flesh) turn out to be used by God for his purposes. This should not surprise us, as God has an infinite capacity to bring good out of evil. The mystery will come into the open when the man of lawlessness talked about in the previous verses is revealed. "Lawlessness" refers to disobedience to God. But it is limited in operation by what is first referred to as a restraining force ("what is restraining him"), and then openly as a personal being ("he who restrains").

The concept of rebellion against God being "restrained" in this present church age is directly confirmed by the statement in Rev 20:2 that the work of Satan is "bound" during the millennium. This has been accomplished by the work of Christ at the cross, which is reflected in Jesus' statement that he would bind the strong man (Mk. 3:27). And this in turn demonstrates that what Revelation describes as the "millennium" is directly equivalent to the present church age that extends from the resurrection to Jesus' return. This is the time when, according to Jesus, Paul and John, Satan is bound or restrained, until that time at the end of the millennium and shortly before the return of Christ where the restraint is removed ("after that he must be released for a little while," Rev. 20:3). The binding of Satan, as the New Testament affirms, refers to a divinely-directed limitation of Satan's powers, so that the message of the gospel can effectively go forth to every nation and receive a response in the hearts of all those God has chosen. From Babel to Pentecost, the nations of the world were cast out by God and placed under the rulership of demonic spirits, but from Pentecost onward, God has purposed to take the chosen of all nations (people groups) back for himself.

To understand this better, we need to take a tour back to the early history of the human race. After the flood, the earth was gradually repopulated by the descendants of Noah, who spread out over vast distances. Among these was Nimrod, described as a *gibbor* or mighty man, like the *nephilim* of Gen. 6:4. The *nephilim* may or may not have been fallen angelic figures, but in any event are not cast in a positive light, and the terminology used in the text links Nimrod with them. Significantly, Nimrod became the founder of Babel or Babylon, the literal and symbolic center of evil in the Bible. Nimrod plays a significant role in the mythology of ancient Babylon. The founding of Babylon is thus linked back to the story of the giants and the judgment of God on the world through the flood. So it is no surprise that the third major judgment of God upon humanity (after Adam and the flood) falls upon Babel or Babylon. And this in turn points to the significant fact that the last judgment of God also falls upon Babylon and her allies (Revelation chapters 17-20).

This ancient judgment is reported in Genesis 11: "Come, let us go down and there confuse their language" (Gen. 11:7). The people of the earth had joined together to make a name for themselves by building a tower to reach to where they conceived the dwelling of God was. The implication is that they were challenging God's rulership and attempting to establish their own. As a judgment, Yahweh confused their language and scattered the nations over the face of the earth (verse 9). Immediately following this comes the story of God's taking Abraham out of the heart of the Babylonian homeland. Moses gives his commentary on the events of Babel, "When the Most High gave to the nations their inheritance, when he divided mankind, he fixed the borders of the peoples according to the number of the sons of God. But the Lord's portion is his people, Jacob his allotted heritage" (Deut. 32:8-9). God scattered the nations, then chose Israel. The fact that God chose Abraham means that God effectively disinherited the other nations. And in doing so, he abandoned them to the rule of demonic powers who blinded their eyes to the reality of the one true God. Satan and his agents were operating freely — "unbound" — but never outside of God's ultimate authority.

But all this was reversed by the work of Christ on the cross. The significance of this fact becomes clear in Luke's account of the events of Pentecost. At Pentecost, Jews and Gentile converts from all over the Roman world were gathered together in Jerusalem. Each of them heard the praises of God being spoken, and no doubt at the heart of it was the good news about Jesus. According to verse 6, they were "astounded" or "astonished." The same verb, which can also mean "confuse," is used twice in the Greek text of Genesis 11, where it refers to the confusion of the tongues at Babel. God brought confusion at Babel, but brought astonishment at Pentecost. This use of terminology cannot be an accident. *It demonstrates deliberately that the tongues of Pentecost undid the damage of the tongues of Babel.* At Babel, which means Babylon, God dispersed the nations and sentenced them to idolatry and bondage to demonic spirits, while choosing one man out of Babylon, Abraham, through whom to build his covenant people. At Pentecost, God undid the curse, and released the power of the kingdom to every nation. The ungodly unity God cursed at Babel is replaced by the divine unity that draws people of every nation together in Christ. God's judgment on the nations of the world is lifted through the finished work of Christ, and the ability of Satan and his agents to deceive the peoples of those nations is now curtailed. This does not, of course, mean that every person will be saved, but rather that those God has chosen before the foundation of the world (Eph. 1:4) will respond to the gospel message. *This is the binding of Satan*, which will continue throughout the church age until a time shortly before the Lord's return. The commission to extend the boundaries of the kingdom that both Adam and Israel failed to fulfill will be accomplished by the church until the gospel of the kingdom has gone to every nation (Mt. 24:14, Mk. 13:10).

This panorama of Biblical history brings us to the identity of the restrainer, for it is the restrainer, according to Paul's teaching, who enforces the binding of the devil and his agents. Who, then, is the restrainer? The answer comes from looking at the Biblical background influencing Paul's thinking in this passage. As we noted in the last chapter, he has spoken of the man of lawlessness, and this figure seems to be based on the ancient enemy of God's people prophesied in Dn. 9:27, "And on the wing of abominations shall come one who makes desolate, until the desire end is poured out of the desolator,"and again in Dn. 11:36, where he is described as one who will "exalt and magnify himself above every god, and shall speak astonishing things against the God of gods." This links the Daniel figure not only to Paul, but to Jesus' prophecy of the abomination of desolation, which was in one sense fulfilled in AD 68. However, in Paul's thinking, as we have noted, this is only a foreshowing of a similar but more sinister and powerful figure, the man of lawlessness, arising in the very last days before the return of Christ. This identification is reinforced by the mention in Dn. 12:3 that in the last days, after the book of prophecy is unsealed (12:3), the righteous will be purified and the wicked will act *lawlessly* (12:10). According to Revelation 5, Jesus unsealed that book at his resurrection and ascension, and so Daniel's latter days (Dn. 2:28-29, 45) are inaugurated by the work of Christ. The time of the present working of lawlessness under divine restraint is the church age, though the time of restraint will come to an end.

Daniel also introduces another significant figure in the context of this battle against demonic forces, the archangel Michael, who is presented as the pre-incarnate Christ's helper (Dn. 10:13, 21), and as the "great prince" in charge of God's people (Dn. 12:1). Michael is thus presented as the "patron saint" of God's people. That is why it is so significant that Michael appears in Rev. 12:7 as *the principal agent fighting against the dragon at the time of the death and resurrection of Christ.* Let's sum up the evidence. Michael is identified as the patron saint and protector of the people of God in these passages from Daniel, which can be linked to both Jesus' teaching on the abomination of desolation and to Paul's teaching on the man of lawlessness or antichrist. Michael is also linked closely in Rev. 12:7-9 to the casting out of Satan from heaven which *initiates the time of Satan's binding or restraining.* We conclude from this that the restrainer Paul refers to here is to be identified as none other than the archangel Michael. When God removes Michael's restraining role, the enemy will emerge from the bottomless pit (Rev. 11:7) for one last but futile battle against Christ and his church.

CHAPTER NINE

THE LAST CONFLICT AND THE FALL OF THE ANTICHRIST

As noted in chapter seven, both Christ and the antichrist are described as having a "coming" or *parousia*. This is the only time in the Bible that the word *parousia* is used of anyone other than Christ. The *parousia* of the antichrist is described in the next verse, "The coming (*parousia*) of the lawless one is by the activity of Satan, with all power and false signs and wonders…" (2 Thess, 2:9). A *parousia*, as explained in chapter three, occurs when a ruler arrives outside a city, and the citizens come out to escort him back into the city and declare their allegiance to him.

This comparison reveals three things. First, the antichrist is pictured as a person who makes a personal arrival just as much as Christ. Second, the end goal of both comings is to establish a rule on earth, whether of Christ or antichrist, not to take followers out of the earth. Third, the antichrist is a demonic mimic or copy of Christ. Revelation sets out the same kind of theme in relation to the Satanic mimicry of the trinity consisting of the dragon (mimicking the Father), the beast (mimicking the Son) and the false prophet (mimicking the Holy Spirit). We discuss this further in chapter twelve.

Three times in this passage, the lawless one is said to be "revealed" (verses 3, 6, 8). Use of a verb in the passive form is a common way in the New Testament of portraying the hand of God at work behind the scenes. In other words, it is God who does the revealing. The same idea can be seen in the phrase "a thorn *was given* me in the flesh" (2 Cor. 12:7), or "that he may grant you to *be strengthened* with power by his Spirit (Eph. 3:16). It underlines the fact it is God who does the revealing. Meanwhile, the word itself emphasizes the fact that what is to be revealed is *now hidden but still present.* This is in line with the statement of verse 7 that the "mystery of lawlessness is already at work" (verse 7), as well as John's teaching that "while antichrist (singular) is coming, so now many antichrists have come" (1 Jn. 2:18a).

This indicates that the spiritual entity behind these lawless, antichrist forces is at work throughout the church age and uses many individuals to attain its nefarious ends. It also shows that the same spiritual entity will cause an individual of great ability, power and wickedness to arise in the very last days before the return of the Lord to attempt to seize the allegiance of the church from Christ. This is in line with the teaching of Revelation that the dragon, beast and false prophet work through individuals throughout history to oppose the church from without, and corrupt and undermine it from within. The evil work of all three demonic entities from the time of the resurrection onward is vividly described in Revelation 12 and 13.

Christ will destroy this lawless one by the "appearance of his coming" (2 Thess. 2:8). Christ's return is referred to in the New Testament not only by the word *parousia*, but also by the word *epiphaneia*, meaning "appearance". The word *epiphaneia* referred in Greek to a sudden and unexpected occurrence. Just when it seems all is lost, the Lord will return.

Deception, delusion and destruction

Paul continues his teaching, "The coming of the lawless one is by the activity of Satan with all power and false signs and wonders, and with all wicked deception for those who are perishing, because they refused to love the truth and so be saved. Therefore God sends them a strong delusion, so that they may believe what is false, in order that all may be condemned who did not believe the truth but had pleasure in unrighteousness" (2 Thess. 2:9-10).

Evil may be made incarnate in a person, but Satan is the power behind the antichrist figure and controls him. The lawless one comes with all power, and that power is expressed in "false signs and wonders." These are real supernatural activities. They are described as "false" not because they are fake, but because they lead to deception for "those who are perishing." The present tense in the latter phrase shows that this power of deception is already at work along with the spirit of lawlessness, and is already leading people to their doom. However, it will enter into an entirely new phase at the end of the age. The purpose of the binding of Satan at the cross and resurrection (Mk. 3:27), which carries on throughout the church age (Rev. 20:2-3), has as its purpose *the limiting of the enemy's power to deceive* those God has chosen for salvation. Throughout the church age, the Lord opens their hearts to hear the gospel and be saved. This does not, of course, mean that Satan has no opportunity to work his evil purposes, simply that he is limited in what he can do, particularly in opposing the spread of the Gospel.

However, at the end of the church age, the beast will rise from the bottomless pit (Rev. 11:7; 17:8), and be released by God to bring deception upon the lost such that few or none can be saved. This is pictured in the refusal of the lost in the very last days to repent, even in the face of cosmic calamities intended as unmistakeable signs of God's judgment (Rev. 9:20-21). Far from repenting, they will curse God for the pain they have brought upon themselves through their worship of the beast (Rev. 16:10-11). The clear teaching of Paul that the power of deception will be released only in the very last days confirms that the millennium of Revelation 20 is in fact the church age as a whole, not some limited period at the end of it. It is only at the *end of the millennium*, immediately prior to the return of Christ, that the demonic power of deception will be released through the rise of the lawless one or antichrist. Paul's portrayal of the lawless one adds a piece to the puzzle not supplied in Revelation as to how the enemy can operate so powerfully in the period immediately before the return of the Lord.

The calamitous events precipitated by the rise of the antichrist warns us that the days immediately prior to the return of Christ will be marked not only by the spread of the gospel to the ends of the earth, but also by a dramatic Satanic counter-offensive. This time of brief but severe persecution is described at more length in Rev. 11:7-10, "And when they have finished their testimony, the beast that rises from the bottomless pit will make war on them and conquer them and kill them, and their dead bodies will lie in the street of the great city that symbolically is called Sodom and Egypt, where their Lord was crucified. For three and a half days some from the peoples and tribes and languages and nations will gaze at their dead bodies and refuse to let them be placed in a tomb, and those who dwell on the earth will rejoice over them and make merry and exchange presents, because these two prophets had been a torment to those who dwell on the earth."

The events portrayed in Revelation 11 provide the backdrop to the rise of the antichrist figure, and explain how such a man could attain such power. The church, represented symbolically by the two witnesses (chapter six), finishes its "testimony" to Christ at the end of history, immediately before the Lord's return. In 6:11, during the seals vision, John is shown that a time will come when the full number of the saints to be killed is completed, and this verse describes that day. At the time of the completion of their witness, many faithful believers will be killed. Jesus spoke of a time when the church would appear to be defeated, when Christians would be "put to death" and "hated by all nations." This would be a time, he said, when "many will fall away and betray one another and hate one another." At that time, "lawlessness will be increased" and "the love of many will grow cold. But the one who endures to the end will be saved" (Mt. 24:9-13).

The fact that "the beast... arises from the bottomless pit" (Rev. 11:7) does not mean that the beast has no function or power until the very end of the church age. What it means is that, by God's permission, his deceptive activity is allowed to manifest openly and with little constraint at that time. But this apparent release is meant only to expose the power of evil for what it is, and prepare it for its ultimate judgment. The same event is described in Rev. 17:8, where the beast rises "from the bottomless pit" and goes "to destruction." The final warfare of the beast against the saints at the very end of the church age will result in the beast's final destruction.

The same event is described for a third time in 20:7, "when the thousand years are ended, Satan will be released from his prison," only in the end to be thrown into the lake of fire (20:10).

This final warfare against the church will make it seem as though the church is defeated: "Their dead bodies will lie in the street of the great city that symbolically is called Sodom and Egypt, where their Lord was crucified" (Rev. 11:8). In the Old Testament, lack of burial constituted a gross indignity (Ps. 79:1-5; Isa. 14:19-20). At the end of the age, following the glorious expansion of the kingdom to the nations of the earth, the influence of the church will seem to have been suppressed, marginalized or even eradicated owing to the severity of the persecution. The "great city," which in Revelation 17 is portrayed as end-times Babylon, is here compared to Sodom, Egypt and even the Jerusalem which crucified Christ. This city is to be understood *symbolically*, as these multiple references indicate. Babylon and Egypt were the places of the captivity of God's people, and Sodom and Jerusalem symbolize humanity's rebellion and evil. The city is not in any one location, but represents the activity of an evil power in the hearts of rebellious people across the world.

That the event occurs on a worldwide basis is shown again in Rev. 11:9, where it is said that it will be witnessed by "peoples and tribes and languages and nations." This will occur for a period of "three and a half days." This phrase identifies a much shorter period than the *three and a half years* (Rev. 11:3; see 12:14; 13:5) of the witnesses' testimony. The church will proclaim the gospel throughout the church age, but at its very end will face a short period of intense persecution and apparent defeat. The parallel to Christ's ministry is obvious. The three and a half years corresponds roughly to the powerful ministry of Christ on earth, whereas the three and a half days corresponds to the time he spent in the tomb. The church follows in the footsteps of her Lord. This latter apparent but temporary defeat of the church will be a source of rejoicing for "those who dwell on the earth" (Rev. 11:10). "Those who dwell on the earth" is a phrase used throughout Revelation to refer to unbelievers whose judgment comes on account of their persecution of the saints and also on account of their idolatry (3:10; 6:10; 8:13; 13:8, 12, 14; 14:6-9; 17:2, 8).

Let's return now to the passage in 2 Thessalonians 2. Judgment, Paul states in verses 9-10, is coming on the followers of the lawless one. This judgment is entirely deserved, because they have rejected love of the truth (verse 10). The "truth" for Paul is a synonym for the Gospel (2 Cor. 4:2; 13:8; Gal. 2:5, 14; Eph. 1:13). The lost are judged not just for their rejection of the truth, but for their rejection of "love of the truth." The Gospel is not simply an intellectual message. It requires total commitment, accompanied by deep love and devotion to Christ and his message. The love of the lost is directed toward themselves and not God.

This rejection leads to a "strong delusion" sent by God (verse 11a). The phrase in Greek is "the working (*energeia*) of deception." The word *energeia* in Paul refers to a supernatural manifestation, either of God or the enemy. The result is they believe "what is false" (verse 11b), The Greek text here reads "the lie." The presence of the Greek definite article ("the") indicates one specific lie is referred to — we might paraphrase it as "the big lie". The lie may refer to the claim of the antichrist figure to be God, or it may refer to rejection of the fact the Gospel is true. We may find it strange to think that God would place people under a supernaturally-directed delusion. But this has been his way ever since he hardened the heart of Pharaoh. Revelation paints the same picture, where the effect of the various plagues released from the throne of God is to harden the lost in unbelief, so that they refuse to repent, and curse God instead (Rev. 16:21). This is the same reality Jesus referred to as blasphemy against the Holy Spirit (Mt. 12:31), a level of sin from which deliverance is impossible, or the "sin that leads to death" in 1 Jn. 5:16. It is the same thing Paul was describing when he talked of the deliberate and continued rejection of God leading to God "handing people over" to a deep level of sin and "giving them up to a debased mind" (Rom. 1:24-32).

All these things are at work in the present: "For the mystery of lawlessness is already at work" (2 Thess. 2:7). This process of the lost rejecting God and God hardening their hearts in return takes place throughout the church age. But this passage points to a time in which there is a powerful deepening of the battle, precipitated by the arrival of Satan's "superhero," a man with the ability to gain the allegiance of the masses of lost people on a worldwide basis, reinforced by his capacity to work supernatural signs and wonders. This is facilitated by the release of the devil and his agents from the bottomless pit in which they have been restrained since their casting out from heaven at the cross, and their being granted permission by God to lead the lost into a final and fatal deception.

Yet in all this, the bottom line is that the sovereign plan of God is being worked out. The Lord Jesus will be revealed in flaming fire to take vengeance on his enemies and "to be marveled at among all who have believed" (2 Thess.1:10). The antichrist figure and all that he represents will be destroyed in a moment. Even as the saints will be resurrected and transformed "in the twinkling of an eye" (1 Cor. 15:52), so also in that same momentary flash of time the forces of evil will meet their destruction.

That is the both the final line and the bottom line of Paul's eschatology.

CHAPTER TEN

THE MARK OF THE BEAST

Of all the predictions and speculations about the events of the end, the identity of the mark of the beast is always near the top of the list. And it is often massively misunderstood and the source of much unnecessary fear.

The mark of the beast emerges in Revelation as the work of the second beast or false prophet. The false prophet is pictured in Revelation as the demonic counterfeit of the Holy Spirit, even as the dragon is seen as the demonic counterfeit of the Father, and the first beast is portrayed as the demonic counterfeit of the Son. The false prophet is assigned a specific task, "Also it causes all, both small and great, both rich and poor, both free and slave, to be marked on the right hand or the forehead, so that no one can buy or sell unless he has the mark, that is, the name of the beast or the number of its name" (Rev. 13:16-17). The beast is the demonic entity working to use the power of human governments against the church, and here it works with the false prophet to enforce its rule. The mark is equated with both the name of the beast and the number of that name.

But what is the exact nature of the mark? The most important thing we need to know is that the mark of the beast which is identified as the name of the beast and which is written on the foreheads of unbelievers is the *exact satanic counterpart* to the name of God which is written on the foreheads of believers. The two groups are placed in direct contrast to one another, as John moves directly from describing the lost in 13:16-17 to describing the saved in 14:1, "Then I looked, and behold, on Mount Zion stood the Lamb, and with him 144,000 who had his name and his Father's name written on their foreheads."

The names of God and the Lamb "written on their foreheads" are clearly identical to the seal on the foreheads of the same group of people in chapter 7, as is clear from a comparison of the two passages. In 7:1-4, John sees the seal being placed by an angel on the foreheads of the same group of 144,000 people who are to be protected by God. Before harm is done to the earth or those who dwell in it, God's servants must be sealed. John's vision is rooted in the vision of Ezekiel, in which God commands an angel to put a "mark on the foreheads" of those faithful to him before striking Jerusalem in judgment (Ezek. 9:4-6). Ezekiel's vision in turn is based on the mark of blood on the door of the Israelites protecting them from harm during the first Passover (Exod. 12:7, 13, 22-28), and ultimately is rooted in the protective mark on Cain (Gen. 4:15). The vision pictures the church standing at the beginning of a new Exodus, being led into a period of trial and testing, yet one in which it will be protected from spiritual harm by the hand of God.

Both "seal" and "name," therefore, along with the Old Testament equivalent of "mark," carry the meaning of protection and ownership. None of the words are to be understood literally. The seal and the mark are figurative or symbolic ways of signifying ownership, of God's protection of those who belong to him. To be in someone's name likewise denotes ownership. The "name" of the Lord denotes God's ownership of us. That is why we are baptized "in the name" of Jesus (Ac. 10:48), and why God will give us what we ask "in his name" or as those under his authority (Jn. 14:13).

This group of the saved is pictured, as noted above, *in immediate contrast* to the group of those worshiping the beast and with his name or mark written on their foreheads (13:14-17). This indicates clearly that both sets of names and marks, which are placed in direct opposition to each other, are to be understood figuratively or spiritually, rather than literally. Those worshipping the Lamb are owned by God, even as those worshipping the beast are owned by the devil. The mark of the beast is not a literal mark. It is neither a bar code, as predicted in the 1990s, a computer chip (in a vaccine!), as predicted in 2020, or some other kind of invisible electronic identification. And it is something every single follower of the beast has, even as every single follower of the Lamb has the mark of God.

This should be good news for the believer and unbeliever alike. It is clearly possible for the lost to be saved, gain the mark of God and lose the mark of the beast. But the believer has been chosen in Christ before the foundation of the world (Eph. 1:4), has been redeemed by the blood of Christ (Eph. 1:7), and — it cannot be coincidence — has been *sealed* with the Holy Spirit (Eph. 1:13). The lost can rid themselves of the mark of the beast, but those genuinely saved can never lose the mark of God. The two marks are mutually exclusive. No unbeliever can carry the mark of God, and no genuine believer will ever carry the mark of the beast. False end-times teachers have sown massive confusion and fear into the hearts of sincere believers that at any time they could on account of some undefined sin gain the mark of the beast. That is a lie.

The word "mark" (Greek *charagma*) carried a charged meaning for the Christians in the seven churches of Asia Minor. It refers to the seal of the emperor and the impression of his head on coins. This explains the meaning of the statement, "no one can buy or sell unless he has the mark" (Rev. 13:17).

Only those who submitted to the idolatrous practices of the pagan culture in which they lived would enjoy its economic benefits — be allowed to buy or sell. What this means is important to understand, for it is rooted in events of the first century, not the last days before the Lord's return. Bar codes and computer chips have nothing to do with it!

Christians were under increasing pressure to conform to Roman practices of emperor worship. The *charagma* was on the coin. To be identified with the emperor's "mark" or image on the coin was to agree to worship him in exchange for economic benefits. At the time John was writing to the seven churches, the emperor was Domitian, who ruled from AD 81-96. He revived the ancient practice of the imperial cult — worship of the imperial family —and he declared various deceased members of his family to be gods. Some historians allege that he called himself *Dominus et Deus* — Lord and God. Society in Roman times was structured such that those working in any occupation had to belong to trade guilds. Each trade guild was ordered by Domitian to conduct services in which the imperial family was worshipped at various times during the year. Those who refused to participate were ejected from the guild. This effectively reduced Christians to utter poverty, for they were not able to earn an income and there was no modern social safety net. Only those who identified with the emperor's mark and worshiped him were able to participate in the economy — to *buy and sell,* as John phrases it.

This still has relevance for us today. Although we are not asked to worship our political leaders, there are many ways in which we are under pressure to compromise our faith in order to gain acceptance within our culture. These pressures may soon exclude non-compromising Christians from certain areas of employment or social acceptance. Believers are already coming under legal sanction for failing to compromise with certain social beliefs or practices. Like the Christians at Smyrna whose poverty was linked with their profession of faith (2:9), true believers can be expected to suffer economic as well as physical and political persecution. The latter phenomena are visible in many nations of the world today, where the beast has invaded fallen human governments in order to oppress God's people. To reduce this to being tattooed on the forehead with a barcode or implanted with a computer chip in our hand in order to have a Costco membership reveals how ludicrous the dispensational insistence on literal interpretation is, interpreting the Scriptures through symbols of current technology rather than by the clear meaning of the Bible itself.

But why is it that the mark of the beast's ownership is placed on the "right hand or the forehead" (Rev. 13:16)? If the forehead represents our beliefs, the right hand represents our conduct as a result of those beliefs. This is a satanic counterfeit of commitment to God and his law. The law of God is understood in Exod. 13:9 as a "sign on your hand and as a memorial between your eyes [=forehead]." The same idea can be seen in Exod. 13:16; Deut. 6:8; 11:17. The "blasphemous names" written on the foreheads of the first beast, along with its ten diadems, signify its false claims to kingship (13:1). The fact that the beast's name is "written on" unbelievers signifies their agreement with those false claims and their refusal to worship the true God.

The Christians to whom John was writing in the first century were those who carried the mark of God, while unbelievers around them carried the mark of the beast. The same is true today. The mark of the beast has been around since the days of Adam and Eve, and will be until the Lord returns. In his mercy, it is possible for anyone who turns to faith in Christ to lose it. But no genuine Christian — thanks be to God! — can ever gain it.

CHAPTER ELEVEN

THE PLAGUES

I was teaching a course on eschatology in the United States in January 2020 as the first reports of health issues in China were trickling out. I made the statement that this would prove to be a classic example of one of the plagues of Revelation. God would use it to judge an idolatrous world which had placed its trust in medicine and technology, and he would equally use it to confront a church which had become lukewarm and compromised. My statement only sounded shocking to people because they thought of the plagues as events which would not take place until shortly before the Lord's return. A reading of the last book of the Bible shows how mistaken this view is.

Revelation portrays four sets of seven judgments or plagues

brought by God on an unbelieving world during the church age. These numbers are not accidental. Though they are symbolic like every other number in Revelation, their meaning is easily interpreted by the only interpretive grid Revelation exhibits, which is the over 500 allusions to the Old Testament present in its 404 verses. The numbers, like all the sometimes strange figures and events portrayed in the various visions, find a clear explanation in the pages of Scripture — and not in the latest news reports from the middle east! In this case, the number four, which is the number of the earth, and which originates in the four rivers of the garden, is joined to the number seven, which is the number of God and of completion, as in the seven days of creation. The four sets of seven judgments, therefore, represent the complete judgment of God upon the earth.

The judgments consist of the seals, the trumpets, the seven visions of chapters 12-14 and the bowls. In each set, the first four or five judgments describe events throughout the church age, while the last two bring us to the end of history and the inauguration of the eternal kingdom. The last judgment or the inauguration of the eternal kingdom is described four times at the end of each cycle (6:12-17; 11:15-19; 14:14-20; 16:17-21/19:11-21). The four sets of judgments are thus repetitive: they portray the same sets of events but from different perspectives, just as the Gospels do. They are, in significant part, based on the plagues of Exodus. The reason for this is simple. Revelation is a description of a second Exodus, one for which the first Exodus was merely a forerunner. God's people are pictured as leaving the bondage of spiritual Egypt or Babylon, crossing a sea in which a latter-days dragon dwells, being kept safe while tempted in the wilderness for a period of time related (through use of the number 42) to the time the Israelites spent there, and eventually entering the heavenly Promised Land. The sounding of the seventh trumpet, with the ark in full view and an earthquake taking place, marks a latter-days Jericho as God's people enter the Promised Land of the new Jerusalem.

The purpose of these plagues is as it was in the days of Pharaoh. Hardships caused by natural, economic or military forces are used by God to harden the hearts of unbelievers and express a provisional form of judgment. Those whose hearts are open will be awakened by these judgments to turn their hearts to Christ. Those who are already believers are given an opportunity to bear witness and demonstrate their faithfulness, in the assurance that God will use the trials to draw them closer to himself and thus foreshadow their eventual eternal reward.

This raises the question as to how God could be pictured as sending or allowing judgments which affect his own people. The Biblical answer is that, although God is the author only of good, he uses even the trials of this fallen world to work his good purposes in his faithful people. He used even the cross to bring about our salvation. James reminds us to "count it all joy" when we encounter "trials of various kinds," since the testing of our faith in trials produces a good result in that we are "perfect and complete, lacking nothing" (Jas. 1:2-4). Likewise, Peter says that though "we are grieved by various trials," these trials cause our faith to be refined and will result in "praise and glory and honor at the revelation of Jesus Christ" (1 Pet. 1:6-7).

When do these plagues commence? Dispensationalists assume that they occur during a last days seven year period of tribulation, in which Israel is attacked by hostile nations, culminating in the battle of Armageddon. But such a tribulation, as we discuss in chapter sixteen, does not exist. The "great tribulation" of Rev. 7:14 is in fact a description of the church age. If this is the case, we should expect that the judgments of God portrayed in Revelation might well occur throughout this time period. And indeed they do.

But the earlier chapters of Revelation, before the judgments are even mentioned, provides the strongest evidence that our view is correct. As John's vision of God's throne room unfolds in chapters 4-5, he witnesses the fulfillment of the prophecy of Daniel 7 regarding the Son of man coming before the Ancient of Days, "Then I saw in the right hand of him who was seated on the throne a scroll written within and on the back, sealed with seven seals. And I saw a mighty angel proclaiming with a loud voice, 'Who is worthy to open the scroll and break its seals?'" (Rev. 5:1-2). John sees in God's right hand "a scroll written within and on the back, sealed with seven seals". This is an allusion to Ezek. 2:9-10, where the prophet also sees a scroll in God's hand with writing on the front and back. That scroll, as the following chapters in Ezekiel reveal, represents the judgment of God on humanity. This links the Ezekiel passage with Daniel, who also saw books of judgment in the presence of God (Dn. 7:10), shortly after which the Son of man appeared to take his kingdom (Dn. 7:13-14). Daniel was ordered by the angel to "seal the book" recording these divine judgments until "the time of the end" (Dn. 12:4, 9).

The way John's words so closely follow the words of the prophets indicate without doubt that *this is the very scroll that Christ unseals*. Daniel spoke of the kingdom of God which would come to pass "in the latter days" (Dn. 2:28). In the very first verse of Revelation, John quotes Daniel's words but changes them to say the events would take place not in the latter days but "quickly" or "imminently." The meaning is clear: John is announcing the *arrival* of events Daniel expected to occur *in the last days*. There is no doubt John saw the resurrection of Christ as fulfilling the prophecy of Daniel regarding the inauguration of the kingdom of God. For John and for the New Testament in general, the last days commenced with the resurrection and ascension of Christ. The last days (see chapter four) are now.

What John sees next is highly significant. The breaking of the seals initiates the four sets of seven judgments, "Now

I watched when the Lamb opened one of the seven seals" (Rev. 6:1). This breaking occurred *at the moment of Christ's ascension to the right hand of God.* The judgments or plagues started then and have continued ever since. They are not connected with a supposed seven year period prior to Christ's return, but are an integral part of the church age as a whole.

The judgments of the first four seals consist of war, famine, death and plague (Rev. 6:1-8). This fulfills the prophecy of Ezekiel concerning four judgments of sword, famine, wild beasts and plague (Ezek. 14:14-21). The purpose of Ezekiel's trials was to punish the unbelieving majority while purifying the righteous remnant. This prophecy, pertaining to the faithful and unfaithful in Israel, is now universalized to include believers and unbelievers among all nations. Jesus likewise prophesied war, famine and persecution would characterize the years following the fall of Jerusalem, yet would not indicate his return was imminent (Mt. 24:6-8). Jesus warned believers to endure during these difficult times, which would affect them as well as unbelievers. Both Ezekiel and Jesus presented these judgments as occurring alongside each other. This suggests the trials should not be seen as isolated incidents which take place one after the other, but rather are generally characteristic of the entire period in which they occur. The time from Christ's resurrection until his return will thus be marked by recurring periods of such varied judgments. Suffering presents an opportunity for Christians to find their strength in God, even while the hearts of those around them are being further hardened.

The trumpet judgments and the bowl judgments are based closely on the plagues of Exodus, with the significant difference that they are to be taken symbolically, rather than literally. This should not surprise us, given what we have seen of the meaning of Biblical symbolism in Revelation. The fact that they are symbolic, however, does not mean they have no actual application.

The first trumpet features hail, fire and blood and is modeled on the plague of hail and fire (Exod. 9:22-25). Here we see God's judgment on the world's weather and climate systems, where such judgment bring havoc on nations across the world. The second and third trumpets feature the poisoning of the sea and the waters, and are modeled on the plague on the Nile (Exod. 7:20-25). The sea was the main channel of commerce then as it is now, and this plague represents judgment on the world's commerce and economy. The fourth trumpet brings darkness, just as did the Egyptian plague (Exod. 10:21-23). Darkness brought literal confusion to the Egyptians, and this plague speaks of God's judgment on the false ideological and philosophical systems which bring the world into intellectual and spiritual confusion. The fifth trumpet involves locusts, like the original plague (Exod. 10:12-15). This represents judgment on the world's agricultural economy, without which people cannot survive.

The bowls are not literal bowls, but represent the judgments of God poured out on the world. There is a great similarity between the trumpets and the bowls. The bowls portray the events of world history in the same way as the trumpets, though with some variations of detail. The bowl judgments emphasize more consistently the fact that the plagues fall upon hardened unbelievers dwelling in the kingdom of the beast, who practice idolatry (16:2), refuse to repent (16:9, 11) and persecute Christians (16:6). The bowls (16:5-7), like the trumpets (8:3-5), represent the answer to the prayers of the saints for justice as recorded in 6:9-11. Both trumpets and bowls present the plagues in the same order. They both strike (in sevenfold sequence) the earth, the sea, the rivers, the sun, the realm of the wicked with darkness, the Euphrates, and the entire world with the final judgment. They are both accompanied by lightning, sounds, thunders, earthquake, and great hail. Both trumpets and bowls are rooted in the Exodus plagues. The plagues of Exodus serve as typological judgments, prophetically foreshadowing the plagues of the church age and culminating in the final judgment of the wicked.

The purpose of the plagues was not so much to cause the Egyptians to repent as to demonstrate their hardness of heart and the rightness of God's judgment against them, and to release that judgment. According to Exod. 4:21, the plagues were sent to harden Pharaoh's heart with the result that he would *refuse* to let the people go. This in turn would release the judgment of God against Pharaoh and his nation (Exod. 7:3-4). Most importantly, however, the plagues were sent simply so that God himself would be glorified over all the gods of Egypt (Exod. 7:5; 8:10). The same pattern plays out in the bowl judgments. The Exodus plagues turn out to be prophetic forerunners of these judgments. Although some may repent, the ultimate purpose of the judgments is the hardening of the hearts of unbelievers and the bringing to pass of God's judgment. The overriding goal of the judgments, however, is to glorify God and demonstrate his authority over the nations of the world.

The unsealing of these judgments at the ascension of Christ means that we should expect them to occur from time to time throughout history. They can be regional or global. When they are global, as in the case of the 2020 pandemic, we should wake up and take note. While God is judging the world, his primary concern is with his church. The letters of Revelation reveal several of the churches in poor or dire spiritual condition. Only two, in fact, were doing well. If we as individual Christians or as church communities come through a season of global shaking and come out of it the same as we were before, we are ignoring God's warning at our peril. Awake, and strengthen what remains!

CHAPTER TWELVE

666

Few other topics in Biblical eschatology have seized the popular imagination more than this three digit number, in spite of the fact it makes only one brief appearance in the Bible (excluding an Old Testament reference to the weight of Solomon's gold). Here is that statement, "This calls for wisdom: let the one who has understanding calculate the number of the beast, for it is the number of a man, and his number is 666" (Rev. 13:18). What could be the identity of this nefarious figure? Speculation in recent times has reached a fever pitch, but it is by no means a modern phenomenon. One author compiled a list of over one hundred names identified as 666 in literature published between the sixteenth and nineteenth centuries.

Many attempts, as you can imagine, have been made to interpret the meaning of this number. Almost all of them have involved the use of "gematria," a system used in ancient languages, including Greek, Latin and Hebrew, which substituted letters of the alphabet for numerals. Each number stood for a letter. We still employed Latin gematria until fairly recent times for numbering bullet points (i=1, iv=4, x= 10, and so on) or even gematria based on the modern alphabet (a=1, b=2, etc). Our modern numerical system is actually a product of medieval Arabic mathematicians.

The problem for us is that gematria does not provide any clear identification linking 666 with a particular name which would fit the context. In other words, there are lots of names in various languages whose combination of letters add up to 666, but none of them are potential candidates constituting a Biblical villain. With gematria, you can *turn any name into a number*, but it's another thing to come up with one name that fits the context of Revelation *from a number*. In spite of hundreds, if not thousands, of attempts over the centuries at altering spellings and adding titles to potential viable candidates, nothing has come of any of them. One writer on the subject pointed out that such writers, in a desperate attempt to prove their case, add titles to the name, switch languages and find non-existing spellings.

The most common candidate for identifying 666 is Nero, who ruled from AD 54-68. The reason for this is that Nero fits a certain interpretation of the text, in this case the preterist interpretation. Preterists seek to prove that virtually all the events in Revelation, in particular, the persecution and suffering of the church, occurred prior to the destruction of the temple in AD 70. They identify the cosmic signs of Revelation and the Gospels (the falling of the stars from the sky, the sun and moon being darkened) as fulfilled in their entirety in the destruction of Jerusalem by the Romans — an interpretation which stretches credulity, to say the least. The problem for them is that the portrayal in Revelation of a suffering church does not fit their triumphalist view that the church will rule the world before Christ returns. Hence, they want to confine the church's suffering to the first century.

So to identify Nero, a first century Roman emperor who launched the cruel suppression of the Jewish rebellion in AD 66, as the beast is critical for preterists. But here is where the mischief begins in the use of gematria. First of all, a language that fits is chosen, in this case Greek, rather than Nero's own language Latin. Then one title (out of many Nero had) is arbitrarily added, in this case *Neron Kaisar* (a transliteration of the Latin *Nero Caesar* —note the change of spelling from Latin to Greek!). Next, the name is transliterated from Greek into Hebrew — *Neron Kaisar* in Hebrew letters. Finally, the Hebrew spelling is changed by adding the Hebrew letter *yodh* (i) into the Hebrew transliteration of the word *Kaisar*, even though there is not a single example of the word being spelled that way in all of Hebrew literature. Then magically, once all these changes have been made, the gematria adds up to 666. And many preterist Bible teachers claim to have solved the puzzle. Remember, of course, that John was writing in Greek, not Hebrew, and many of his readers would not have had any familiarity at all with the Hebrew language. And then finally there is the small detail that it was not Nero (who died in AD 68), but his successor Vespasian who conquered Jerusalem in AD 70.

In the last century, and particularly since the turbocharging of dispensationalism that took place as a result of the founding of the state of Israel in 1948, things have once again taken off in the world of predicting candidates for this numerical demon, who is usually conflated with the Antichrist, whether by use of gematria or not. This time, names of individuals alive at the time of the person making the prediction have been suggested — and all of them in due course discarded, due to the decease of the individual involved. These have included Kaiser Wilhelm, Adolf Hitler, Henry Kissinger, Saddam Hussein, various Russian dictators and a medley of popes. Some of these personalities were indeed operating on the dark side, though others were clearly chosen by people simply because they disliked their political views. All such attempts fail, however, for one simple reason: *they do not understand the symbolic use of numbers in Revelation.* All of these numbers (think of the 24 elders, 4 living creatures, 7 seals, trumpets and bowls, 2 witnesses, 4 winds, 4 horses and riders, 7 heads, 10 horns, 1000 years and so on) receive their meaning by reference to the text of the Old Testament. *Numbers are given meaning not by gematria or other means, but by their Biblical significance.* Why would 666 be any different? The Bible has an amazing way of interpreting itself, if we will only allow it to do so.

But another question arises. Is a person even being referred to? According to 13:17, the mark of the beast is the same thing as "the name of the beast or the number of its name." In chapter ten, we saw that bearing the mark and name of the beast signify being owned by the beast, in the same way that having the seal or name of the Lamb signify being owned by the Lamb. *Both the name of the beast and its number constitute his mark written on the foreheads of the lost.* Two verses later, in 14:1, believers are pictured with the *name of the Lord written on their foreheads*. The name of the Lord refers to a supernatural spiritual reality (God or Christ). The name or number of the beast must refer to the opposing demonic reality (Satan or the beast). This is exactly what we saw in chapter ten. *No human being, alive or dead, can therefore be identified with 666, which is instead to be identified with the supernatural powers of darkness.* We give further reasons for this below.

This is supported by a correct understanding of the phrase "for it is the number of a man" (13:18). This phrase has often been misinterpreted to mean that a particular individual is referred to, who is then generally identified with the antichrist or man of lawlessness. However, John does not use the definite article ("the") before "man." The correct translation is, "for it is the number of humanity." Or more specifically, because of the context of reference to ownership by the beast, the number of fallen humanity. It is the number of *humanity as fallen* because fallen humanity is under the ownership of the devil and his agents. *If a specific individual were in mind, the definite article "the" would have been used.*

How then are we to understand the number? If the number seven (used repeatedly in Revelation) refers to completeness and to God, it is God's number. The number six, by contrast, is the number of fallen humanity. Humanity was created on the sixth day, but unlike God, is incomplete — without the seventh day of rest we would not have come to completion. Adam and Eve did reach that completion, yet lost it when they fell. Six is hence the number of fallenness, rebellion and the one who instigated that rebellion. The sixth seal, the sixth trumpet and the sixth bowl portray God's final judgment on the followers of the beast, whereas the seventh component in each series portrays the eternal kingdom of Christ, or a judgment which ends in the establishment of the eternal kingdom. The use of three sixes points to a level of fallenness beyond that of fallen humanity. *It points to the demonic reality out of which fallen humanity emerged.*

Chapter 13 reveals the demonic trinity of the dragon, the beast and the false prophet. The three sixes signify the demonic counterfeit of the Trinity (the dragon, the beast and the false prophet) and the fallen humanity that demonic trinity controls. In support of the concept of the demonic trinity, consider the following parallels:

The beast as counterfeit of the Son. The Son receives authority from the Father (2:27; 3:21), while the beast receives authority from the dragon (13:4). The beast has crowns (13:1), and so also does Christ (19:12). The beast appears as slain and is resurrected (13:3), as is also the case with Christ (1:18; 5:6). The Son of man steps forward to receive kingdom authority from God, as a result of which people from all tribes and nations serve him as his kingdom advances in power (5:6-14; Dan. 7:13-14). The beast rises to receive kingdom authority from the dragon, as a result of which the whole world and its fallen expressions of government follow him (13:1-3).

The second beast or false prophet as counterfeit of the Spirit. The Spirit is the breath of God (Gen. 1:1; Jn. 20:22; Ac. 2:2). The false prophet gives breath to the statue of the beast (13:15). The Spirit glorifies the Son (Jn. 16:14). The false prophet glorifies the beast (13:12-15). The Spirit empowers the church to bear true witness and be the instrument for the advancement of God's kingdom (Ac. 1:8). The false prophet empowers unbelievers to use ungodly religious institutions to advance the kingdom of darkness and counteract the true witness of the church (13:11-18).

John begins this verse with a warning: "this calls for wisdom." This warning puts believers on guard against the continual deceptive work of the beast throughout history. We need God's wisdom to interpret the Bible. Yet such a task should not be difficult. The Bible is not meant to be so complicated that no one can understand it. Given that no one else has yet been able to come up with a concrete historical identification for 666, we should not be surprised if dispensationalists of the future might resort to a twenty-first century supercomputer! But John is not posing a complex mathematical problem for us. The real solution is one every believer from John's day until now can easily grasp. He is pointing to a reality which any Spirit-filled believer can readily understand: the work of Satan and his agents is present among fallen humanity in every age, even within the visible church, and must be guarded against with all possible vigilance.

But just in case you're interested in gematria — the Greek word for "beast" (*therion*), when translated into Hebrew, turns into 666. Maybe there's something to it after all! The beast, it turns out, is the beast.

CHAPTER THIRTEEN

THE 144,000

Revelation has no shortage of numbers, and none are without significance. But as we've seen, we have to turn to the Bible itself to figure out what that meaning is. The group of 144,000 saints appears twice, in 7:4-8 and 14:1. The Jehovah's Witnesses teach this is the elite group who by their service to the cult will make it to heaven, while the rest of the Witnesses will live in an earthly paradise. Darby taught it was the literal number of Jews who would be saved in the tribulation. Dispensationalist teachers often picture this as a group of 144,000 Jews who are protected by God in the tribulation in order to evangelize those left behind after the church has been raptured. Dispensationalist teacher Tim LaHaye, author of the Left Behind series, referencing Rev.14:4, claims these evangelists are all Jewish male virgins! But if we work on the assumption that the answer is to be found in the Old Testament, none of these odd interpretations need be accepted.

The vision John sees is described as follows: "And I heard the number of the sealed, 144,000, sealed from every tribe of the sons of Israel: 12,000 from the tribe of Judah were sealed, 12,000 from the tribe of Reuben, 12,000 from the tribe of Gad, 12,000 from the tribe of Asher, 12,000 from the tribe of Naphtali, 12,000 from the tribe of Manasseh, 12,000 from the tribe of Simeon, 12,000 from the tribe of Levi, 12,000 from the tribe of Issachar, 12,000 from the tribe of Zebulun, 12,000 from the tribe of Joseph, 12,000 from the tribe of Benjamin were sealed (Rev. 7:4-8)." Note the exclusion of Dan and Ephraim from the list, which suggests a literal reference to the tribes of Israel is not in view here. This may be because both Dan (Jdg. 18:16-19; 1 Kgs. 12:28-30) and Ephraim (Hos. 4:17-14:8) were associated in the Old Testament with idolatrous practices, which is often warned against in Revelation.

In the second half of chapter 7, John sees "a great multitude that no one could number" (verse 9), which is identified as "the ones coming out of the great tribulation" (verse 14). There is a pattern in Revelation where first John hears something and then he *sees* what he has *heard*. For instance, in 1:10 he hears a voice, and then in verse 12 he sees the person who is speaking. In 5:5, he hears of the Lion of Judah, and then in verse 6 he sees the Lamb. In 5:1, he hears the living creature summoning something, which he then sees in verse 2 as a white horse, the same pattern recurring with the other three horses in that chapter. *In all these cases, what is first heard and then seen are the same thing.* And here in 7:4, he first *hears* of a group of people, then in verse 9 he *sees* them. That means the two groups are one and the same. He hears of the group by means of their numerical symbolism in the Bible, in this case the people of God, then he sees the actual multitude.

This makes sense when we see that the identity of the 144,000 is based on the fact that every number in Revelation is symbolic rather than literal. It does have concrete meaning, but that meaning is determined by its reference in the Old Testament, rather than anything our own modern minds might conjecture. This is clearly the case here. The number twelve represents the people of God, and is squared. The squaring includes the faithful saints of both old and new covenants, the twelve tribes representing the old covenant and the twelve apostles representing the new. The resulting number, 144, is then multiplied by a factor of one thousand, which represents a very large indefinite number, as in 2 Pet. 3:8 ("a day is as a thousand years"). The 144,000 thus represent the indefinitely-large number of God's faithful people throughout history, both old covenant and new, both Jew and Gentile. This makes sense when we see that the same idea is conveyed in 21:13-14, where *the twelve tribes and twelve apostles together* form the foundations of the new Jerusalem, whose walls rise to a height of *144 cubits.* If the whole redeemed people of God are pictured here, this makes even more sense in light of the significance of the fact they carry the seal (7:4). In light of 2 Cor. 1:22; Eph. 1:13 and 4:30, the seal is surely to be identified with the Holy Spirit. The sealed are the saved of all ages, for Paul states clearly that all believers have been sealed with the Spirit.

This is corroborated by the other passage where the same group of 144,000 appears. In 14:1, the group is pictured as standing on the heavenly Mount Zion with the Lamb, with the name of God and of the Lamb written on their foreheads. The fact that the group were sealed according to chapter 7, but are described instead as having the name written on their foreheads in chapter 14, means that the seal of chapter 7 and the name of chapter 14 must be identical. The name in the Bible signifies ownership, and so does the seal. Paul writes, "But God's firm foundation stands, bearing this seal: 'The Lord knows who are his.'" (2 Tim. 2:19). By contrast, the earth-dwellers have on their foreheads the mark of the beast, which is likewise his name (13:17; 14:9-11), signifying their ownership by the beast. The seal on the saved and the mark on the lost are thus both symbols of ownership, not literal marks, as we've noted in previous chapters.

Two groups are contrasted by John, those with the name or mark of the beast (13:17-18) and those with the name or seal of the Lamb (14:1-4). The first group without doubt represents the lost of all time, and the second equally represents the saved of all time. *All* Satan's followers bear his mark or name, and *all* the Lamb's follower's bear the Lamb's mark or name. If this is true, then it must be the case that all of God's people of every tribe and nation and every stage of history must be considered as sealed, all have the name of the Lamb written on them, and all are thus are to be included in the symbolic number of the 144,000. This is further confirmed by looking at the wider context of Revelation. In 5:9, it is said that Christ "ransomed people for God from every tribe and language and people and nation." The same group of 144,000 are said in chapter 14 to have been "redeemed from the earth" and "redeemed from mankind" (14:3-4). That is, they have been redeemed or ransomed from the nations of the earth. This undoubtedly identifies the 144,000 with all believers in Christ.

And before this chapter finishes, what about that army of Jewish male virgins Tim LaHaye was talking about? The 144,000 are described as "these who have not defiled themselves with women, for they are virgins" (Rev. 14:4). We've already established that the 144,000 is not a group of latter-day Jewish unmarried male evangelists, but rather refers to the entire group of the redeemed of all ages. Why, then, does John describe them in such an apparently strange way? In the context of Revelation, the answer is simple. The sexual allusion is chosen because of the image of the Babylonian prostitute in chapters 17 and 18. Believers are warned (2:14; 20-23) against committing sexually immoral acts (the Greek word is *porneia*) with the beast-controlled system represented by this harlot. They are, in this sense, to be virgins. They are pictured as male simply because the harlot is pictured as female. The concept of *porneia* includes participation in the whole Babylonian system, with a particular emphasis on moral compromise in order to achieve economic and social gain, and thus to avoid hardship and persecution. So if Christians engage in activities related to Roman emperor worship in order to participate fully in the local economy, they would be committing *porneia.* The kings and merchants of the earth are pictured as committing *porneia* with the harlot through their profiting from her economic activity (17:2; 4; 18:3, 9; 19:2).

The portrayal of believers as virgins should not be surprising, because the church is presented in Revelation as a bride clothed in white linen betrothed to Christ (19:7-9 and 21:2). Paul likewise writes to the Corinthians: "I betrothed you to one husband, to present you as a pure virgin to Christ" (2 Cor. 11:2). The Old Testament similarly refers to "virgin Israel" (2 Kgs. 19:21, Isa. 37:22, Jer. 14:17; Lam. 2:13, Am. 5:2). The issue of the army of latter-days Jewish male virgin evangelists shows us once more the strange places dispensationalism leads us to when it disconnects phrases from the rest of the Bible — as well as common sense.

CHAPTER FOURTEEN

ARMAGEDDON

Like 666 and the millennium, Armageddon is mentioned in only passage in the entire Bible. The advantage we have in figuring out what it (and the other two) mean is that the one occurrence is in Revelation. Revelation, as we've noted, is saturated with over 500 allusions to the Old Testament in its 404 verses, more allusions than all other books of the New Testament combined. That means we have another resource to draw on. And as we'll see, it pays off.

The mention of Armageddon comes in one of the six places in Revelation which allude to the final battle between good and evil. During the days of the sixth bowl judgment, three unclean spirits are released by the demonic trinity of the dragon, the beast and the false prophet. They dry up the Euphrates and go forth to the "kings of the whole world" to "assemble them for battle on the great day of God the Almighty." The account continues, "And they assembled them at the place that in Hebrew is called Armageddon" (Rev. 16:16).

There are actually two Greek words in the text, *har Magedon*, or the "mountain of Megiddo." A number of Old Testament prophecies state that the prophesied eschatological battle will take place at Jerusalem (Joel 2:1, 32; Mic. 4:11-13; Zech. 12:1-5; 14:1-5, 13-14). Yet Megiddo was a two day's journey from Jerusalem — which can hardly be described as even a suburban part of the city. Not only that, Megiddo is a plain, and the present site of Megiddo sits at most on a very small rise of land, whereas the Hebrew word *har* refers to a mountain. It's clear that the reference is not to a literal geographical location.

John is likely combining two significant places in Old Testament history into one symbolic location. The plain of Megiddo was the site of two famous battles (Judg. 5:19; 2 Kgs. 23:29; 2 Chron. 35:22). It became a symbol in Judaism for the place where righteous Jews were attacked by wicked nations. Eventually, it also became for the Jewish people a prophetic symbol of the last battle. In the conflict with Barak and Sisera, God said he would "draw out" Sisera (Judg. 4:7) to the "waters of Megiddo" (Judg. 5:19). In the same way, God now gathers the pagan kings for battle at the mountain of Megiddo. At Megiddo, the righteous King Josiah was defeated by the Pharaoh (significantly portrayed in the Old Testament as a dragon) on his way to the Euphrates — and it cannot be coincidence that the very same river is mentioned in just a few verses earlier in Rev. 16:12. Megiddo, in the Jewish mind, was a place of great significance. The mountain (*har*) referred to is likely Mount Carmel, which was not far from Megiddo. Mount Carmel was the location of another of the Old Testament's greatest battles between good and evil (1 Kgs. 18:19-46). There Elijah (symbolic of the church in Rev. 11:3-7) defeated the prophets of Baal.

John joins the two somewhat close but separate locales into one symbolic place — the mountain of Megiddo or (in Greek transliteration) *har Magedon*, transliterated into English as Armageddon. Consider the parallels between these two Old Testament references and John's Armageddon. Both feature the defeat of kings oppressing God's people (Judg. 5:19-21; Rev. 16:14; 19:17). Both feature the destruction of false prophets (1 Kgs. 18:40; Rev. 19:20). Even though Josiah is considered a "good" king, both feature the death of kings who are misled or deceived (2 Kgs. 23:29; 2 Chron. 35:20-25; Rev. 16:13-14).

The purpose of the enemy's deception is to "assemble them for battle" (Rev. 16:14). The same battle or war is referred to in 19:19, where the beast, the false prophet and the kings are "gathered to make war." It is also the battle mentioned in 20:8, where Satan and the nations of the world are gathered "for battle." The three synonymous phrases (16:14; 19:19; 20:8) are based on Old Testament prophecies that God would gather the nations together for the final war of history, "I will gather all the nations to Jerusalem to battle" (Zech. 14:2; see Zechariah chapters 12-14; Ezek. 38:2-9; 39:1-8). The three parallel references in Revelation are all prefaced by the definite article ("the"). This gives a different nuance to the meaning of the phrase. It is not just "for battle" but rather "for *that* battle." It is for *that war of the end,* the war the Bible has prophesied and that all pious Jews know about, because it is prophesied by Ezekiel and Zechariah. Given that the three passages in chapters 16, 19 and 20 all refer back to "that" battle the prophets were foretelling, it means that *all three passages are referring to the same war*. This will have great significance for our understanding of the millennium. The battle of 20:8, which takes place at the *end* of the millennium, is the same battle alluded to in chapters 16 and 19. This proves that the millennium itself covers the *same time period* as that ending in the great battle of chapters 16 and 19 -- namely, *the church age*.

Armageddon is thus *a symbolic representation of an undefined place where the last battle between good and evil is to take place.* Zechariah places the battle at Jerusalem, though the primary reference here, as the wording in verses 19:17-18 makes clear, is to Ezek. 38:2-9 and 39:2. Ezekiel refers to the last battle occurring not in or near Jerusalem at all, but on the mountains of Israel (38:7-9; 39:1-8). In fact, Ezek. 38:16 sees the whole land of Israel being the battleground. This shows that even the prophets did not have one clear locale in mind. They were using the reality in front of them — the land of Israel — understanding it to represent the dwelling place of God's people. The path to determining what Israel and the dwelling place of God's people refers to is found in the context of how both Revelation and the New Testament as a whole interpret the Old Testament prophetic promises (see chapter nineteen). In this light, it is significant that, in both 1:6 and 5:10, John sees the promises made to Israel through Moses as fulfilled, through Christ, in his church composed of both Jews and Gentiles. Paul expresses exactly the same idea in Rom. 2:27-29; 9:6-8; Gal. 4:21-31; 6:16. The dwelling place of God's people is wherever his church is gathered.

Armageddon is identified in symbolic (though real) terms as the place where the eschatological battle against "the camp of the saints and the beloved city" (Rev. 20:9) takes place. The saints in the New Testament are without exception identified as followers of Christ, and the beloved city is surely the church, as understood by Paul as the "Jerusalem above" (Gal. 4:26) and Hebrews as the "heavenly Jerusalem" where believers in Christ dwell. The text in Rev. 16:12-16 thus identifies Armageddon in a worldwide perspective as signifying the final battle against the church. The divergence in terminology in the prophetic literature helps us to see that Ezekiel and Zechariah were themselves not pointing us to one literal place.

One further point of interest is that Zechariah identifies the day of the last battle as a "unique day, which is known to the Lord, neither day nor night" (Zech. 14:7). On that day, "living waters shall flow out from Jerusalem" (Zech. 14:8). These are surely the same living waters Ezekiel saw coming from the new creation temple (Ezek. 47:1-12), described by John as the living waters flowing from the throne in the new Jerusalem (Rev. 22:1-2). Something far more than a geographical location in the middle east is clearly being referred to!

CHAPTER FIFTEEN

IS THE CHURCH IN THE BOOK OF REVELATION?

One of the foundation stones of dispensational Biblical interpretation is the assertion that the rapture took place prior to the beginning of the visionary section of Revelation. This allows for the events unfolding in chapters 6-19 to be understood as a depiction of a latter days tribulation in which a restored Israel is being attacked by the forces of the Antichrist. Yet there is absolutely no evidence in the text of Revelation to support such a position.

Dispensational interpreters such as John MacArthur, in his book *Christ's Prophetic Plans*, justify their position on what is called an argument from silence, specifically that the church is not present because the church is not mentioned. To begin with, and for obvious reasons, arguments from silence are considered one of the weakest forms of argument. To build a massively significant and controversial interpretation of Scripture on such an argument is risky, to say the least. Yet are there any grounds for the assertion itself? We contend there are not.

To begin with, to suppose that the church is not mentioned in Revelation simply because the word "church" (*ekklesia*) does not appear in it is a rather weak contention. The word *ekklesia* does not appear in other New Testament letters either, such as 2 Timothy, 1 and 2 John and Jude. No one would seriously suggest that the church is absent there. Neither is the word "church" mentioned in chapters 21-22. Are we to suppose on this basis that the church is excluded from the new creation? Even dispensationalists would not say that. And after chapter 7, there is no mention of "Israel" in the text either. If, on the basis of the argument from silence, the church was raptured after chapter 3, we must assume on the basis of the same argument that Israel likewise was raptured after chapter 6. This alone shows the impossible nature of the dispensationalist position.

But let's look back at our discussion of the 144,000 in Revelation 7. There we worked carefully though the evidence and came to the conclusion that the text refers not to a group of latter day Jewish male virgin evangelists, as suggested by dispensational teacher Tim LaHaye, but rather to the church of all ages, Jew and Gentile alike. So it's not the church, but rather Israel that isn't mentioned in Revelation!

But if we need more evidence, we have it. The letters and the visions are far more closely linked than is often realized. The reason this is the case is because the visions portray *present-day realities in the life of the church and the world*, not just events immediately prior to the Lord's return. Revelation must be understood as relevant to every generation, including that to which it was originally written, and not only to the last generation before the return of Christ. All this underlines the fact that *Revelation is a pastoral letter written to the churches*, even though it includes such rich prophetic elements. It therefore makes sense that the present-day realities of the letters reappear in the visions.

For instance, the believers at Smyrna will endure a brief persecution (2:10), as will those in the vision slain for their faith (6:11). The believers at Philadelphia will receive spiritual protection in the midst of tribulation (3:10) and the names of God and Christ will be written on them (3:12). In the same way, the faithful saints in the vision are sealed and protected against harm (7:3). They likewise have the names of God and Christ written upon them (14:1). Antipas at Pergamum is God's witness (2:15). So are the believers in 6:9 and the two witnesses in 11:3-13. Satan has his throne at Pergamum, where he is accompanied by a false prophet (3:13-14). Satan reappears in the visions as the dragon thrown out of heaven who has established his rulership (throne) on earth and is accompanied by a false prophet (12:9; 13:13-14; 16:13). Jezebel is in the church at Thyatira (2:20-22), but reappears as a model for the Babylonian harlot (17:2-3). In particular, every promise made to faithful believers in the seven churches is fulfilled in the new Jerusalem (the tree of life, freedom from the second death, the new name, and so on).

Above and beyond this, the church is pictured as priests to God in 1:6, and again in the visionary section at 5:10 and 20:6 (interestingly, in the millennium). The church is pictured bearing witness to Christ and his word in 1:2, 9, and again in the visions in 6:9; 12:17; and 20:4 (again in the millennium). The church experiences patient endurance in Jesus in 1:7, and again in the visions in 13:10; 14:12.

And what about the "the camp of the saints" which is being attacked at the end of the millennium (20:9)? The term "saints" is often used in the Old Testament to refer to the wilderness encampment of Israelite tribes around the tabernacle. The same encampment imagery of the Pentateuch, according to G.K. Beale in his longer commentary on Revelation, is applied in Rev. 20:9, except now the Israelite imagery is applied to the church existing at the conclusion of history. In the New Testament, the word "saints" (Greek *hagioi*) is applied no longer to Israel but to the church. As early as the book of Acts, the word is used to describe the members of the first Christian churches (9:13, 32. 41; 26:10), and is never used to describe unbelieving Jews. *I am not aware of anywhere in the New Testament where the noun "saints" is used to describe the non-Christian Jewish community.* The closest would be use of the word as an adjective in the Gospels in the term "the holy city," which was simply a common way of referring to Jerusalem.

This strongly suggests that in Revelation, where the word is used thirteen times, it refers to the church there also. The fact that the camp of the saints is equated with the beloved city in 20:9 adds further support to this. In Rev. 3:12, in the section addressed to the church at Philadelphia, it states that all Christians of every race and nation *will have the name of this city, Jerusalem, written on them.* The walls and foundations of this city have the names of the twelve tribes *and* the twelve apostles written on them (21:12-14). This shows that the beloved city is composed of believers of all ages, including faithful saints of both old and new covenants. Although the new Jerusalem is an eternal reality, it is also present in an incomplete way now, which is why it can be referred to in 20:9 as an earthly reality. Paul clearly identifies the "Jerusalem above" with the church (Gal. 4:26), as opposed to the "present Jerusalem" (Gal. 4:25), which is ethnic Israel, pictured as being in slavery. Heb. 12:22 teaches that believers in Christ have already come to "the city of the living God, the heavenly Jerusalem." *Spiritual Jerusalem, the camp of the saints, is the worldwide body of Christ.*

Revelation begins and ends by affirming it is a pastoral letter written to the churches of Asia Minor (1:4; 22:16). Like all the other letters of the New Testament, its content, while it extends far beyond this boundary, must also be applicable *to those to whom it was written.* That is one of the most basic canons of Biblical interpretation. The dispensational alternative strains all credulity by asking us to believe that the letter written to the seven churches does not in general apply to the seven churches, and further, that those to whom it does apply are a group of Jewish unbelievers in a seven year period at least two thousand years in the future.

The idea that the church is not in Revelation has no basis in the text of Revelation, or indeed in the text of the New Testament as a whole, and exists for one reason only — to perpetuate the myth of a non-existent rapture.

CHAPTER SIXTEEN

THE TRIBULATION

The tribulation and the millennium are perhaps the hardest concepts to explain, in no small measure because the way dispensationalists have contorted Scripture requires a lot of untangling. I've left these chapters to the latter part of the book, and while I've made them as understandable as possible, you might want to take some extra time reading them over.

The tribulation according to Jesus

There are three parallel passages in the Gospels where Jesus describes the events of the end times — Matthew 24, Mark 13 and Luke 21. For the sake of simplicity, we'll work here from Matthew's account, which is the longest and most detailed. In these accounts, we find Jesus' understanding of the tribulation. All three begin with Jesus telling the disciples about the forthcoming destruction of the temple which took place, as Jesus indicated, within the lifetime of his listeners: "Truly, I say to you, this generation will not pass away until all these things take place" (Mt. 24:34). These accounts are important, for Bible scholars agree that they form the basis for Paul's teaching on eschatology in 1 and 2 Thessalonians. Jesus himself sets the pattern for the church's eschatology, as D.A. Carson points out in his commentary on Matthew (*Expositor's Bible Commentary*, vol. 9).

According to dispensationalism, Jesus' reply to the disciples has nothing at all to do with the destruction of *that* temple, the one they were explicitly asking about. Rather, in verses 4-25 the long discourse he gives is not about a coming time of trial the disciples will witness within their lifetime, or even the lifetime of their most distant descendants. He speaks instead of a seven year tribulation at least two thousand years in the future, to take place immediately prior to his return. *He speaks of the destruction not of the temple the disciples are asking about, but of an end-times temple rebuilt by the antichrist they know nothing about.* The disciples *think* he is answering their question about the imminent destruction of the temple they see in front of them, but, *unbeknownst to them*, he is really describing another destruction of the same city millennia in the future. The disciples could not possibly have understood Jesus' teaching this way, and this interpretation makes Jesus out to be a complete deceiver.

To understand the passage properly, it is necessary to notice the way Jesus talks in the passage about two entirely different sets of events or periods of time. On the one hand, he describes events which will take place throughout the church age, including specific events which will occur within the lifetime of the disciples and will fulfill Biblical prophecy. On the other hand, he also refers to events immediately surrounding his return. Making sense of the passage requires us to notice the distinction Jesus makes between these two periods of time. It is important to note, as Carson again points out, that the verbs used in the New Testament in connection with the Lord's return (waiting for, watching, expecting) all include the idea of some kind of delay, and many passages *clearly rule out* the imminency of the Lord's return, as occurs in this chapter at verses 45-51 (see also Mt. 25:5, 19; Lk. 19:11-27; Jn. 21:18-19; Ac. 9:15; 22:21; 23:11; 27:24). What the Bible does teach us is to be ready, if only because we do not know the hour the Lord may call us into his eternal presence.

Mt: 24:4-14

Jesus begins by warning of events which will take place, *but will not signify the times of the end.* This segment (verses 4-14) is a general description of the church age. It includes false Messiahs (verse 5), and the classic Old Testament trio of disasters signifying God's ongoing judgment of rebellious people — wars, famines and earthquakes (verses 6-7). Then he says this: "All *these* are but the beginnings of the birth pains." He continues to elaborate on these preliminary events by warning that as they unfold believers will be delivered up to tribulation and death (verse 9). Here we have an immediate indication that the term "tribulation" (*thlipsis*) is connected with the church age. False prophets will arise, lawlessness will increase and the love of many will grow cold. The end of this age will not come until "this gospel of the kingdom" is "proclaimed throughout the whole world as a testimony to all nations" (verse 14). It is not unreasonable to see this as a description of the church age as a whole. On the one hand, Jesus is describing events that the disciples will personally experience. His statement, "they will deliver *you* up to tribulation," certainly includes them (verse 9). Mark adds the detail that they will be delivered to councils (the Greek word is *sunedria*, referring to the first century Sanhedrin) and beaten in synagogues (Mk. 13:9). Yet on the other hand, this period of events also refers to times far distant in the future, things that have not happened even in our day, because it does not end until the gospel has reached "all nations" (*ethne*, verse 14). Several thousand such groups, as missions organizations will testify, are still unreached even today. In summary, tribulation is seen as a characteristic of the entire church age.

Verses 15-21

The next paragraph contains a further exhortation to the disciples regarding *particular events they themselves would witness*, culminating in the fall of Jerusalem and destruction of the temple. Jesus begins by announcing that his disciples will personally witness the fulfillment of Daniel's ancient prophecy regarding the "abomination of desolation" which was prophesied to take place in the Jerusalem temple ("the holy place," verse 15). Many Jews regarded the desecration of the temple by the Syrian king Antiochus Epiphanes in 167 BC as the fulfillment of this prophecy, though they saw further fulfillments in actual or attempted desecrations by the Roman general Pompey in 63 BC and the Emperor Caligula in AD 40. Yet Jesus saw another, even worse desecration coming. When in AD 68, the Zealots desecrated the temple by committing murder in its precincts and installing a false high priest, the Christian community took it as the fulfillment of Jesus' prophetic warning (verses 16-20) to flee in haste to the mountains and leave everything behind. This event had to happen at some point *before the destruction of the temple* when the Sabbath law was still in effect: "Pray that your flight may not be in winter on a Sabbath" (verse 20). The flight of the Christians took place *en masse* and in great haste in the last days before the Romans stopped allowing people to leave the city. They literally fled to the mountains across the Jordan, and were thus saved from the holocaust that occurred when the Romans destroyed the city and its people. This event is foretold by Jesus to be "a great tribulation" (verse 21), unparalleled until that moment in Jewish history, and never to be equalled. It is true that far greater numbers of Jews perished over a longer period of time and in a much larger geographical context in both Nazi Germany and Russia. However, as Carson puts it, there was "never so high a percentage of a great city's population so thoroughly and painfully exterminated and enslaved as during the siege of Jerusalem." Note that when Jesus says, "and never will be," he is clearly implying an extended future period of time before his return. And history has shown that to be correct. Lk. 21:24 clarifies further that the first century fall of Jerusalem is described here, for he adds the statement, "They will fall by the edge of the sword and be led captive among all nations, and Jerusalem will be trampled underfoot by the Gentiles, until the times of the Gentiles are fulfilled." The "fulfillment" of the times of the Gentiles is clearly identical with the latter days "fullness" of the Gentiles referred to by Paul in Rom. 11:25, which comes near the end of the church age.

Verses 22-28

The next section begins at verse 22, and resumes the description in verses 4-14 of the church age as a whole. It might seem that the phrase "and if those days had not been cut short" refers to the previous discussion about the fall of Jerusalem. But Jesus says the days are cut short "for the sake of the elect." The "elect" in verses 24 and 31 is a reference to all Christian believers, so it seems that here Matthew is transitioning back to his more general description of the church age he began in verses 4-14. Here Jesus makes a prophetic declaration that the church age will end in a divine intervention on behalf of God's people. The same scenario is pictured in Rev. 11:4-13: as the church (represented by Moses and Elijah) finishes its witness in severe persecution, the Lord comes to resurrect the saints and commence judgment. Jesus reiterates his previous warning (verse 5) that this age will be characterized by false Messiahs as well as false prophets, and that false predictions of his return will lead many astray (verse 24). Surely we have seen this come to pass! But when the Son of Man comes, his return will not be a private or secret event (verse 26) but rather one visible to the whole earth (verse 27). His concluding phrase, "Wherever the corpse is, there the vultures will gather" (verse 28) states the obvious: you cannot miss his return any more than a vulture can miss the prey sitting right in front of him.

Verses 29-31

A major turning point arrives at verse 29. The period of tribulation (*thlipsis*) identified with the church age in verses 9 and 22 has come to an end. Jesus begins to talk about the time immediately prior to his return. We know this because of the presence of the cosmic signs of verse 29 — the stars falling from heaven and the darkening of the sun. These are the same signs as those in Rev. 6:12-13, which clearly portray God's judgment at the end of this world. The eschatological meaning of this section is confirmed by the mention of "the sign of the Son of Man" which appears in heaven (verse 30a), which is to be understood as a standard or flag which, along with the sounding of the trumpet (verse 31), is associated in the Old Testament with the end-times victory of God's people ((Isa. 11:12; 18:3; 27:13; 49:22; Jer. 4:21; 6:1; 51:27). Appearance of this sign will cause the nations of the earth to mourn over their rejection of the Messiah as they witness the coming (*parousia*) of the Son of Man on the clouds of heaven (verse 30b). The word *parousia* refers in the New Testament to the coming of Jesus at the end of the age and time of the resurrection of the dead ((1 Cor. 11:26; 15:23. 52; 16:22; I Thess. 3:13; 4:14-17; 2 Thess. 1:7; Jas. 5:7-8; 2 Pet. 1:16; 1 Jn. 2:28; Rev. 1:7). The mourning of the nations is an expression of regret, not repentance, much like the panic that seizes the lost at the world's end in Rev. 6:16-17. The clouds on which he comes are not to be understood as a vertical descent from the upper atmosphere, but rather indicate the presence of God: think of the cloud of glory in the wilderness, and at the tabernacle and temple. The same picture is painted by Paul in his description of believers meeting Jesus in the clouds at his return (1 Thess. 4:17).

The passage so far seems to establish fairly clearly that *the tribulation is to be identified as the period of time from Jesus' resurrection to his return* (the church age). Within this greater *thlipsis* there occurs a brief but extreme *thlipsis* (verse 21), associated with the fall of Jerusalem and destruction of the temple in AD 70. All this is described in verses 4-28. Then, just as clearly, the account moves on in verses 29-31 to a description of the events immediately prior to the visible (and only) return of Christ.

Dispensationalists provide an entirely different, much less credible explanation of the passage. The mention of the *visible* return of Christ in verses 29-31 cannot, they admit, refer to the secret, invisible return invented by Darby under the influence of Margaret MacDonald's ecstatic vision. They therefore take this to refer to his second, visible return which they believe will take place at the end of a seven year tribulation period supposedly prophesied by Daniel (see our explanation of this below). This means, as we noted at the beginning of our discussion, that nothing prophesied by Jesus in verses 4-28 can be taken at face value, that is, as *a description of the church age described as a time of tribulation.* Rather, it refers to *a seven year tribulation at the very end of history which the text itself does not identify as such,* and to *destruction of a temple the disciples knew nothing about and were not asking about.*

This means that Jesus is not answering the question the disciples actually asked, which was concerning the fate of the Jerusalem temple. It means that his answer was highly deceptive, because the disciples (and anyone reading the text ever since) would most certainly have understood him to be talking about the temple they were asking about, the temple right in front of them.

Verses 32-35

The difficulties for dispensationalists continue as the passage progresses. In these verses, Jesus tells the disciples *when* the events they have been asking about will occur. He makes this statement, "This generation will not pass away until all these things take place" (verse 34). According to dispensationalists, "this generation," which the disciples *would certainly have understood to refer to their own generation*, is in fact *the generation alive at the time of an end-times seven year tribulation following an (unmentioned) rapture,* all of which is two thousand years and counting in the future. The temple to which he was referring was a temple built following the rapture during the first half of the tribulation period with the help of the antichrist. By this logic, of course, the *actual destruction* of the temple and Jerusalem, which did take place *within one generation,* and which seems to be clearly predicted here, was in fact something *Jesus apparently knew nothing about*. And the Christian community who fled Jerusalem because they interpreted what Jesus said at face value somehow just got lucky, as it turns out they had completely misunderstood what Jesus was saying and mistakenly taken it as relevant to them. Jesus was so fixated on a non-existent end-times tribulation he apparently missed the real one!

What Jesus does say is this, "So also, when you see all these things, you know that he [or "it"] is near, at the very gates.

Truly, I say to you, this generation will not pass away until all these things take place" (verses 33-34). Let's take what Jesus says here phrase by phrase. "When you see all these things" must refer to the disciples as witnessing the tribulation he has described, which leads to the destruction of the temple. "This generation" is clearly the generation Jesus was addressing, the disciples and their contemporaries. What, then, is the meaning of "he is near" [or "it is near," as the Greek can mean either]? Luke, whose wording in this section is otherwise very similar to Matthew's, records Jesus as saying it is the "kingdom of God" which is near. If Jesus is indeed referring to the temple's destruction, and if the kingdom of God means (as it does Biblically) the rule, reign and power of God, Jesus is telling us that *the reign of God is manifest in the destruction of the temple*. It is another way of speaking of the judgment of God that came upon the Jewish people for their rejection of the Messiah. It is not that God is the author of death or destruction, it is that God takes the actions of sinful humanity (the Jewish Zealots or the Roman armies) and uses them to fulfill his purposes.

Verses 36-51

Jesus now pivots once again from the events of the present generation to the events of the very last days before his return. The contrast is stark. It is expressed by the opposition of "these things" and "that day". The same contrast, expressed by "these" and "those/that", is present in Mark and Luke.

One set of events is predicted clearly by Jesus to take place within a specific time frame, and the disciples are given signs of its occurrence: when they see the armies gathering around Jerusalem and the temple desecrated, it is time to flee. But now Jesus moves to a completely different time and set of events which are by contrast totally unpredictable. No one knows about them, "not even the angels in heaven, nor the Son, but the Father only" (verse 36). These are events which are not predictable, and in fact will catch people by surprise. Just as it was in the days of Noah (verse 37), it will come upon them as they are going about their daily business, "eating and drinking, marrying and giving in marriage" (verse 38). Jesus sums these events up in a warning: "Therefore you must also be ready, for the Son of Man is coming at an hour you do not expect" (verse 44).

Many dispensationalists explain this as a reference to the rapture and find in it their justification of a secret return. The problem is that *Jesus is referring to an unknown hour, not an invisible or unknown event.* The text does not say Jesus' return is *secret or invisible*, simply that it is *unpredictable*. Whenever Jesus refers to his returning, he makes it clear it is a highly visible event known to all. And there is a further problem for dispensationalists. If we understand Jesus' words on the basis of the analogy of Noah's flood as given in the text (verses 38-39), those who are taken in verses 40-41 *are the lost, not the saved.* It is the saved who are left behind!

But if the rapture is so central to Biblical eschatology, why would Jesus not teach explicitly about it, in the same way he teaches explicitly about his second and visible return? The answer, according to dispensationalists, is that the rapture was not revealed until the time of Paul! After all, the Gospels are applicable only to the Jews, and the rapture does not involve the Jews, so why should they know about it? *This raises the question as to whether Jesus, unlike Darby, was fully aware of the rapture himself!* The truth, of course, is that, though the disciples Jesus was speaking to were undeniably Jews, they were also the very foundation of the Christian church. And Jesus knew more of the mind of God than Darby or any of us.

Jesus also uses the word *thlipsis* in one or two other places. In Matt. 4:18, he speaks in the parable of the sower concerning tribulation which will continually arise on account of commitment to the word of God. In John's Gospel Jesus speaks of the tribulation of childbirth (16:21). And listen to Jesus' words of comfort regarding the normal Christian life: "In the world you will have tribulation. But take heart; I have overcome the world" (Jn. 16:33).

The tribulation, according to Jesus, is part of the experience we undergo in the period between his resurrection and his return. If Jesus laid the foundation for eschatology, we should expect the rest of the New Testament to reflect the same truth. And it does.

The tribulation according to Revelation

At the beginning of Revelation, John addresses the believers to whom he is writing with these words, "I, John, your brother and partner in the tribulation and the kingdom and the patient endurance that are in Jesus, was on the island called Patmos on account of the word of God and the testimony of Jesus" (Rev. 1:9). Only one Greek article ("the") precedes all three words "tribulation," "kingdom" and "patience". What this means grammatically is that all three are considered part of the same reality. *The kingdom is characterized by tribulation and patience.* Christians exercise kingdom rulership characteristically in trial, testing and patient endurance. John's use of the word "tribulation" here indicates that he was already experiencing it, and that the churches with whom he was a "brother and partner" were experiencing it in the context of the first century. There is no reason to assume that the same condition will not apply to believers through the ages. The word is used again in 2:9, 10 to refer to a time of tribulation experienced by the church of Smyrna. Interestingly, it is never used in Revelation in connection with the time immediately before the Lord's return, even though the description in chapter 11 of a severe persecution during that period would easily lend itself to the word being used. The word also appears in 2:22, concerning the tribulation into which God will throw the false prophet of Thyatira.

The church in Philadelphia is given the assurance that they

will be kept from "the hour of tribulation that is coming on the whole world" (3:10). Dispensational interpreters such as R.L Thomas, in his commentary on Revelation 1-7 (1992), argue that this is a reference to the pre-tribulational rapture of the worldwide church. The phrase "the whole world," however, is probably not to be taken as a reference to the whole world in our sense of the phrase. In Lk. 2:1 it refers to the Roman Empire, and in Ac. 11:28, 17:6, 19:27; 24:5, it refers to a more localized area, a usage similar to that found in Jewish literature. Thomas also argues that the Greek phrase "I will keep you from" (*tereso ek*) implies a physical snatching out of, which supports a rapture theory. But the only other place in the New Testament where the same phrase occurs is in Jn. 17:15, "I do not ask that you take them out of the world, but that you keep them from the evil one." Here Jesus is explicitly denying a physical removal from tribulation, but affirming that he will keep believers in the midst of it. Furthermore, it is a stretch to suggest that the phrase "to keep you from tribulation" means physical removal from the world rather than simple protection from trouble that takes place in the world.

The main point to be made, however, is that this is something Jesus is speaking to the church at Philadelphia while John was on Patmos. It is a tribulation the Christians at Philadelphia will live to see themselves delivered from *in their lifetime.* It is a specific promise given to the first century church at Philadelphia *as a reward for their own faithfulness.* Why would John inform these early believers of a deliverance Christians two thousand years or more later would experience? To be sure, God still often delivers believers from trial, and will continue to do so, but that does not nullify the primary reference of the text to those to whom it was written.

A very significant occurrence of the word is found in 7:13-14, "These are the ones coming out of the great tribulation. They have washed their robes and made them white in the blood of the Lamb." Use of the definite article ("the") in Greek adds emphasis. So this is not just *any* tribulation, but *one specifically alluded to in the Scriptures.* It is *that* tribulation you all know about. The phrase "the great tribulation" is in fact drawn from the prophecy of Dn. 12:1: "And there shall be a time of trouble, such as never has been since there was a nation till that time." The 144,000 believers John sees in the vision of chapter 7 represent the entire body of deceased believers (as we explained in an earlier chapter). Therefore, "the great tribulation" must represent the entire church age, exactly as Jesus described it in Matthew 24.

The tribulation according to Paul and other writers

Here we can only give a brief survey. The word *thlipsis* is used 24 times in Paul's writings. Of the 24 occurrences of the word, *22 are used with reference to the present experience of believers in the church age* (Rom. 5:3 (twice) ; 8:35; 12:12; 1 Cor. 7:28; 2 Cor. 1:4 (twice), 8; 2:4; 4:17; 6:4; 7:4; 8:2, 13;

Eph. 3:13; Phil. 1:17; 4:14; Col. 1:24; 1 Thess. 1:6; 3:3, 7; 2 Thess. 1:4). The other two uses (Rom. 2:9 and 2 Thess. 1:6) describe the tribulation which is part of the wrath of God in the final judgment. Not a single use of the word in Paul is used to describe a period of time in the very last days before the return of Christ.

The same is true in Heb. 10:33 and Jas. 1:27: tribulation refers to our present Christian experience.

In summary, from Matthew to Revelation, the New Testament consistently teaches that tribulation or "the great tribulation" (Rev. 7:14) is a characteristic of or simply another term for the church age.

The roots of the fictitious seven-year tribulation

If the word "tribulation" in the New Testament refers to the entire period of time from Pentecost to Christ's return, we might well ask where on earth the idea of a seven year latter-days tribulation came from. The dispensationalist assumption that chapters 6-19 of Revelation represent this seven-year period is *read into the text* and has no foundation in the book of Revelation itself which, prior to chapter 6, clearly characterizes the tribulation *as having already begun in the days of the apostle John and the seven churches*. Nor does it find support in one single verse of the entire New Testament.

Darby and his heirs drew the idea from a twisted interpretation of Dan. 9:24-27. Here is the text:

24 "Seventy weeks are decreed about your people and your holy city, to finish the transgression, to put an end to sin, and to atone for iniquity, to bring in everlasting righteousness, to seal both vision and prophet, and to anoint a most holy place. **25** Know therefore and understand that from the going out of the word to restore and build Jerusalem to the coming of an anointed one, a prince, there shall be seven weeks. And for sixty-two weeks it shall be built again with squares and moat, but in a troubled time. **26** And after the sixty-two weeks, an anointed one shall be cut off and shall have nothing. And the people of the prince who is to come shall destroy the city and the sanctuary. Its end shall come with a flood, and to the end there shall be war. Desolations are decreed. **27** And he shall make a strong covenant with many for one week, and for half of the week he shall put an end to sacrifice and offering. And on the wing of abominations shall come one who makes desolate, until the decreed end is poured out on the desolator."

No one, in fact, would draw the idea of a seven-year end-times tribulation from this text unless that idea had *previously been read into the text* and assumed as correct. This becomes evident from examination of what Daniel wrote. A careful reading of these four verses shows the following:

(1) Daniel prophesied a period of time specified as "seventy

weeks" commencing in a decree to restore and build Jerusalem (Dn. 9:25).

(2) Daniel further identified the *beginning* of this time period with the *end* of the seventy year period of judgment of Israel prophesied by Jeremiah (Dn. 9:2; Jer. 25:14). This is confirmed by Ezra 1:1, which links the decree of Cyrus with the fulfillment of Jeremiah's prophecy and thus constitutes the beginning of the seventy weeks. This period of seventy years is identified as a Sabbath rest for the land, and it is ended by the decree of Cyrus to build the house of God in Jerusalem (2 Chron. 36:21-23). The decree went forth in 538 BC.

(3) This means that the starting point for the 70 weeks is 538 BC.

(4) So what does the 70 weeks refer to? If one week of years is 7 years, then 70 weeks is 490 years. But prophetic numbers in the Bible are generally symbolic (universally so in Revelation), and this is no exception. How do we then find the meaning of the symbolism? In this case, it's not hard. The purpose of the 490 years (seventy weeks = seventy times seven years) is stated as providing forgiveness (Dn. 9:24). In other words, it is *an escalation of the year of Jubilee, which was seven times seven years or 49 years.* The Jubilee was the year all debts were forgiven. This escalated Jubilee year is marked by the complete forgiveness of sins. *That cannot be anything other than a reference to the work of Christ.* That

proves the number is symbolic, while at the same time full of meaning. The Messiah is said to be cut off after 69 weeks, which, if taken literally (69x7= 483 years following the decree of 538 BC) would land Jesus' death in 55 BC, making no sense. This difficulty is avoided if we see the seventy weeks as a symbolic number referring to the time of Jubilee, in which sin is forgiven once for all.

(5) The attaining of ultimate forgiveness in the escalated Jubilee (the death and resurrection of Christ) is followed by the destruction of Jerusalem (Dn. 9:26b, 27b), also prophesied by Jesus (Mt. 24:1-2). At the end of the 69th week, the Messiah will die (be "cut off," verse 26a). Then, "the people of the prince who is to come shall destroy the city" (verse 26b). The people are the Romans, and the prince is Titus, commander of the Roman armies under the emperor Vespasian, at the destruction of Jerusalem in AD 70. This will set off an indefinite period of time characterized by war and desolation, "to the end there shall be war. Desolations are decreed" (verse 26). This period is the church age, just as Jesus described it, one full of "wars and rumours of wars" (Mt. 24:6).

(6) Following his death, the Messiah will "make a strong covenant with many for one week" (verse 27a). This seventieth week is the church age, *neatly making up the entire period of the escalated Jubilee.* It is divided into two parts. The first half of the week involves the Messiah putting

"an end to sacrifice and offering" (verse 27b). This refers to the cross initiating the new covenant in Christ. The end of sacrifice and offerings could either refer theologically to the end of their function in God's economy, or literally to the end of the sacrificial system that occurred with the destruction of the temple, or both.

(7) The second part of the seventieth week takes us to the end of time and the destruction of the desolator (verse 27c), either the devil or one of his servants, exactly in line with Paul's teaching concerning the man of lawlessness. If this time gap seems odd, consider that Peter did exactly the same thing in his interpretation of Joel's prophecy at Pentecost. He moves seamlessly from the outpouring of the Spirit (Ac. 2:17-19) to the events of the end (2:20-21), without any break. Because the numbers are interpreted symbolically (but given specific meaning through the Old Testament allusion to the Jubilee), the fact that the seventieth week spans the entire church age makes sense, as the church age as a whole is the escalated year of Jubilee.

The dispensationalist view

(1) The dispensationalist interpretation hinges on interpreting the 70 weeks as literal years, but to do this and make the numbers work, it requires *abandoning the clear Biblical connection to the decree of Cyrus* and casting around for another event which might work better. This they find in the

later decree of Artaxerxes to rebuild the city (Ezra 7:11, in the year 444), from which a literal 69 weeks times seven yields either AD 32 or 33, but only on the incorrect assumption that one year for Daniel was 360 days or 12 lunar months. The crucifixion, however, is generally dated around AD 29, so the timing is close but not accurate. Our modern calendar assumes 365 day years, and 69 x 7 years (483 years) starting from 444 BC yields a date of AD 39, which is far too late to fit the date of the crucifixion. The Jewish year, on the other hand, has an average of 354 days, which yields AD 25, a date far too early. The problem with the mathematics is obvious.

(2) Remember that Daniel himself places the beginning of the 490 years in 538 BC at the exact end of the seventy year period of judgment of Israel prophesied by Jeremiah (Dn. 9:2; Jer. 25:14). Dispensationalists argue, however, that the decree of Cyrus cannot be used as the starting point, because the prophecy of Dan. 9:25 speaks of a decree to rebuild the city, not the temple, as in Cyrus' decree. But is this argument valid in light of the clear way the Bible links the decree of Cyrus with the beginning of the seventy weeks? The answer is found in the fact that the Jews made no distinction between the city and the temple. Restoration of the temple *assumes* restoration of the city. Daniel had been praying earlier in chapter 9 (verses 2, 16, 18) *in regard to the city, not the temple.* Jeremiah prophesied the desolation of the temple, the city and the land, and his prophecy of the restoration of the people to the land after the seventy years of Sabbath rest

presumes the rebuilding of Jerusalem as well as the other cities, along with the buildings contained therein. The later decree of Artaxerxes was only needed because what was supposed to have been accomplished in the decree of Cyrus fell short, due to the opposition the builders faced.

(3) On the dispensational view, the one making a covenant is not the Messiah, but the latter-day Antichrist. All the events of the seventieth week fall two thousand years and counting after the end of the 69 weeks. But now arises a massive further problem for the dispensational position. That position, you may recall, rests on the assumption that the weeks must be measured not symbolically, as we have done (the 70 weeks = an escalated Jubilee), but rather literally as 490 years (though only as measured by a lunar calendar no one used!). But this in turn *necessitates a massive (so far two thousand year) gap between the literal 69 weeks and the literal seventieth week, whereas there is no such literal gap evident in the text.* It is true, of course, that the view we have suggested must also deal with the idea of a gap, in this case between the first and second half of the seventieth week. But this is far less of a difficulty for our position, in that it defines the 70 weeks as a *symbolic, not a literal number.* The culmination of the promised escalated Jubilee is seen on our view as taking place *in two steps within that week*, its initial fulfillment in the sacrificial death of the Messiah and his resurrection, and the ultimate fulfillment in the Messiah's return and the destruction of the man of lawlessness who

attempts to desecrate the church. *This is entirely in line with the way the prophets foresaw a Messianic deliverance, which the New Testament then clarifies as occurring in this two-stage process of initial and ultimate fulfillment.* It is also exactly what Peter, quoting Joel, preached on Pentecost, when he collapsed the church age into the two stages of the outpouring of the Spirit and the return of Christ, "Even on my male servants and female servants in those days I will pour out my Spirit, and they shall prophesy. And I will show wonders in the heavens above and signs on the earth below, blood, and fire, and vapor of smoke; the sun shall be turned to darkness and the moon to blood, before the day of the Lord comes, the great and magnificent day" (Ac. 2:18-20).

(4) The seventieth week (a literal seven years) is arbitrarily identified by dispensationalists as the "great tribulation" of Rev. 7:14. But this comes up against the fact that that verse in context speaks of the 144,000 saints who have died and entered the presence of the Lord. Given that numbers in Revelation are symbolic (but interpreted by their meaning in the Old Testament), it is clear that this assembly represents the entire group of all deceased saints now in the presence of the Lord awaiting the resurrection — a group of hundreds of millions and rising. The union of the 12 tribes and 12 apostles multiplied equals 144, and this number is further multiplied by 1000, which the Bible uses to indicate an indefinitely large number, which thus yields the 144,000. John "heard of" the group symbolically in 7:1-8 and "saw" it in actuality in the

innumerable multitude of 7:9-17. This suggests that the "great tribulation" is to be identified with the church age, the age from which all these saints have come. And this is confirmed abundantly, just as we have seen, elsewhere in Revelation and the New Testament.

Darby's scheme falls to the ground. The great tribulation is undeniably the church age.

CHAPTER SEVENTEEN

THE MILLENNIUM

Theologians have been divided on the issue of the millennium for as long as the church has existed, though it's fair to say it never became a major or contentious issue until the arrival of dispensationalism. Of those whose views are known to us, the early church fathers, in the second and third centuries, were more or less equally divided as to whether or not there would be an earthly millennium prior to the initiation of the eternal kingdom. Those who believed in the millennium tended also to believe that the souls of the Christian dead rested under the earth in Hades (though in a better compartment than those of the unsaved dead). They would then rise in the millennial kingdom. Those who did not believe in an earthly millennium believed that the souls of the Christian dead went straight to the presence of the Lord, there awaiting the resurrection.

For them, the millennium was identified with the period of time between the resurrection and the return of Christ, during which time the deceased saints were present with the Lord awaiting their resurrection bodies. Partly perhaps because the first view of the intermediate state was far less Biblical than the second, the latter view, best enunciated by Jerome and Augustine in the fourth century, won out and became the prevalent view for most of church history until the nineteenth century. For a description of the views of the earliest church fathers, the very best book to read is an academic study by Charles E. Hill titled *Regnum Caelorum*.

Views of the millennium

Historical premillenialism, the ancient belief in a millennial kingdom, goes back to Justin Martyr and Irenaeus. It sees Christ's return as occurring prior to a thousand year reign on earth. It understands Revelation in a similar way to amillennialism, interpreting it as a picture of the battle between good and evil, in the church age, culminating in a visible return of Christ. It diverges from amillennialism in that it sees Christ then establishing an earthly kingdom in Jerusalem for a literal period of a thousand years, before this transitions into the new Jerusalem, the resurrection of the dead and the final judgment. The primary reason for this understanding is the way in which chapter 20 appears to suggest such a millennial period following the last battle portrayed in chapter 19. This view does not in itself attach any particular significance to the place of Israel, nor does it hold to a latter-days seven year tribulation.

Many credible Biblical scholars and teachers have advocated this view, including George Eldon Ladd, D.A. Carson and John Piper. This view, however, fails to find a cogent Biblical reason for why such a millennium should occur. Why is there need for such a peculiar state, in which unnatural longevity and prosperity occur for those living in its midst? Why would only the last generation of Christians be privileged to enjoy this millennial state? How can this be reconciled with Paul's teaching that all the deceased saints would witness the Lord's return? If only the saved at Christ's return enter the millennial kingdom, the lost having been destroyed at the end of chapter 19, how could there be a further rebellion of the nations when Christ himself is ruling from an earthly throne? As we explore the text of chapter 20, however, we come to the conclusion that John is not referring to a literal millennium at all.

Dispensational premillennialism (commonly known as dispensationalism) is by far the most common form of premillennialism existing today. As explained in the introductory section of this book, this view originated in the serendipitous conjunction of a Bible teacher looking for justification for his views on Israel and a charismatic vision in which God revealed to a teenager in Scotland that Christ was going to return secretly for his church prior to his general return.

According to dispensationalism, as opposed to historic

premillennialism, a much more complicated scenario evolves. First, Christ *secretly* returns and raptures the church to heaven. Further presumed to occur is the resumption of Old Testament sacrifices in a temple rebuilt at the initiation of a personal Antichrist. After this follows a seven-year period of tribulation, half way through which the Antichrist figure will betray the Jews and destroy the temple. This tribulation ends at a *further and this time public* return of Christ (19:11). At that time, Christ will defeat the beast and false prophet (19:19-21), and inaugurate a thousand year reign on earth, based in Jerusalem. The temple destroyed by the Antichrist is rebuilt and the sacrificial system, complete with priests and Levites, is re-instituted, presided over by Christ. Satan is bound (20:1-3), but nonetheless the children of saved believers rebel and so the period ends with the final battle against the devil and his forces (20:7-10). The many reasons we reject this view are discussed at various places earlier in this book. A further and quite substantial reason is discussed as this chapter progresses.

Amillennialism (or, better, ***inaugurated millennialism***) interprets the passage symbolically. It sees both the tribulation and the millennium as referring to the same indefinite period of time which stretches from Christ's resurrection to his return. This period of time is the "church age" in which John lived, in which we live and in which believers in the last generation before Christ's return will live. It exists both on earth and in heaven, where the deceased saints dwell in the presence of the Lord. God's focus during this time is on the church, composed of Jews and Gentiles, notwithstanding his promise in Rom. 11:11-32 to bring a spiritual awakening to the Jewish people before the Lord's return. This view has traditionally been known as "amillennialism," which literally means "no millennium." The term is misleading, however, in that amillennialists *do believe in a millennium*, and that we are presently living in it. It is better termed "inaugurated millennialism." The kingdom is present, but not in its full or consummate form.

Postmillennialism is a form of amillenialism, but with a twist. It sees the millennium as equivalent with the church age, but understands it as trending toward an indefinite period of prosperity and advancement for the church which culminates in Christ's return. Postmillennialists are generally obliged to take a "preterist" (past) understanding of Revelation, interpreting the entire book, save the explicit mentions of Christ's return, as a record of the persecution of the first generation church, culminating in God's judgment of the Jews in the destruction of Jerusalem by the Romans in AD 70. This then removes all the apparent references in Revelation to ongoing tribulation and persecution up until the Lord's return. This interpretation creates an enormous chasm between chapters 6-19, thought to refer to events preceding the fall of Jerusalem, and chapter 20, which catapults us without warning into a description of the triumph of the church in the latter part of the church age. Postmillennialism made its first clear appearance in the seventeenth century, and became popular in the nineteenth century due to optimism surrounding the Second Great Awakening of the 1830s, and even more fundamentally, the general prevalence of the liberal ideas of human progress which permeated the Victorian age. It was championed first by the famous Puritan John Owen, and later by the great Reformed theologian Charles Hodge. Some postmillennialists (B.B. Warfield in particular) even suggested that before the Lord's return, not one unsaved person would be left on earth. After traditional Reformed institutions fell into liberal hands, postmillennialism reappeared in the form of the social gospel, in which social reform was presented as the key to an earthly Christian utopia.

The calamities of world wars and economic depression deflated the postmillennial camp. A minority of Reformed teachers, and a small number of Biblical scholars hold this view today, often combining it with a position called theonomy, the belief that God's laws can and will be imposed on the nations of the earth before the Lord returns. The reliance of this view upon a preterist understanding of Revelation is a major weakness, as we saw in a previous chapter. The New Testament as a whole points to the ongoing reality of tribulation throughout the church age. Revelation indicates that the very last days before the return of Christ will bring difficult and testing days during which the church's very survival may appear to be in question (11:7-10). It is backed up by Jesus' description of the last days as being times of famine, earthquake and war in which his disciples will be hated, false prophets will abound and lawlessness will increase (Mt. 24:3-14). Families will be divided against themselves (Lk 12:53) and will betray one another (Mt. 10:21). Believers will be hated by all, and only those who endure to the end will be saved (Mt. 10:22). The word "tribulation" is used consistently throughout the New Testament to characterize the struggles of Christians in the present age. There is no evidence in Revelation to support a view which suggests the very opposite to be the case.

The millennium in Revelation

The only mention of the millennium in the entire Bible is in the first seven verses of Revelation 20. In verses 1-3, John writes, "Then I saw an angel coming down from heaven, holding in his hand the key to the bottomless pit and a great chain. And he seized the dragon, that ancient serpent, who is the devil and Satan, and bound him for a thousand years, and threw him into the pit, and shut it and sealed it over him, so that he might not deceive the nations any longer, until the thousand years were ended. After that he must be released for a little while" (Rev. 20:1-3).

Because there are no other places in the Bible by which to interpret the term, we have to look at the context in the book of Revelation to gain some clarity. Let's recap a point we made earlier. The clue that the thousand years are to be symbolically interpreted lies first in the use of the verbs "show" and "make known" in 1:1: "The revelation of Jesus Christ, which God gave him to *show* his servant the things that must soon take place. He *made it known* by sending his angel to his servant John." The verb "show" (Greek *deiknumi*) occurs seven times in Revelation. Each time it is used, it refers to the showing of a pictorial vision, which God then interprets symbolically. This meaning is confirmed by verse 1b, where John continues, "He made it known by sending his angel." The verb "made known" translates the Greek verb *semaino*, which means to "symbolize or signify symbolically." This indicates that *the book as a whole* should be interpreted in that manner, including all its numbers. Three numbers in particular, four, seven and twelve, and their multiples, appear many times. They connote the earth or creation (four), the number of God or of completion/totality (seven) and the number of government or God's people (twelve). Why would we assume that the number 1000 would be any different? If we interpret it by other passages such as Ps. 50:10; 91:7 or 2 Pt. 3:8, "With the Lord one day is as a thousand years, and a thousand years as one day", it would seem that the number refers to an indefinitely large number or long period of time.

If that is the case, when does this indefinitely long period of time occur? Our view is that the millennium is a way of referring to the church age, the time between Christ's resurrection and his return. There are a number of reasons for this. The following discussion explains them. It may take you a while to digest these points, but if you want to understand what the millennium is, have some patience and work through them once or twice, with your Bible open in front of you.

(1) You might think that the events of chapter 20 take place after the events of chapter 19. But this is a completely wrong way of reading Revelation. In the book, the visions do not occur in strictly chronological order. John receives a vision and records it *as he receives it*. Some of the visions clearly go back in time relative to previous visions. For instance, the last battle and/or inauguration of the eternal kingdom are mentioned five times prior to chapter 20 (6:12-16; 11:15-19; 14:14-20; 16:17-20; 19:11-21), with subsequent visions going back to a previous time. The vision of 20:1-10 takes us back to a time before the immediately preceding section. The description of the thousand years (verses 1-6) is then followed by a recounting of the final battle between good and evil. If the thousand years refers to the church age, then the final battle described in verses 7-10 must be the *same battle* at the end of the church age described in all the previous passages listed above, and in particular 16:12-16 and 19:11-21. Why is this so? These passages, along with 20:7-10, clearly allude to the *same prophetic visions* of Zechariah and Ezekiel in which the nations of the world are "gathered together" for war against God and his armies (16:14; 19:19; 20:8). The link between the three passages is reinforced by the fact that in each, human armies are gathered together by means of demonic deception, either by spirits of demons (16:14), the beast (19:19) or Satan himself (20:8). In the two previous passages, this battle takes

place *at the end of the church age*. As the same battle is referred to in 20:7-10, it comes at the end of the millennium. The millennium, therefore, must occur *before the end of the church age and the final battle.*

(2) The "first resurrection" of 20:4-5 does not depict a physical resurrection of the saints connected with a millennial period, but is the new birth in Christ. It takes place throughout the church age. To understand this we must go back to the importance of Ezekiel's vision of the dry bones, which Jesus considered so foundational he rebuked Nicodemus for failing to understand it. The fourfold ending of Revelation 20-21 corresponds to the fourfold ending of Ezekiel 37-48: (a) the resurrection of the saints (Ezek. 37:1-14; Rev. 20:4); (b) the coming of God's kingdom (Ezek. 37:15-28; Rev. 20:4-6); (c) the final battle against Gog and Magog (Ezek. 38-39; Rev. 20:7-10); and (d) the eternal Jerusalem or temple, portrayed as a restored garden of Eden and sitting on a high mountain (Ezek. 40-48; Rev. 21:1-22:5). On this understanding, Ezekiel's picture of the resurrection of God's people (the dry bones) *in this context* refers to *the same spiritual reality* as described by Paul in Rom. 6:1-11 and Col. 2:11-12, or by Jesus when he alluded to this Scripture in trying to explain to Nicodemus how we must be be born again. We have been raised with Christ and given a new life through the gift of the Spirit. Hence, the "first resurrection" of 20:4-5 describes saints being born again throughout the church age (buried in baptism and raised in Christ). The *physical* resurrection of

deceased saints, by contrast, occurs at the time of Christ's return (1 Thess. 4:16-17).

(3) Ezekiel sees Gog and Magog as coming from the north (38:6), yet both Rev. 19:15-21 and 20:7-10 universalize them to represent them as the "nations of the earth." This suggests the final battle has nothing to do with events in the region of the middle east. "The camp of the saints and the beloved city" (20:9), which the enemy forces attack, is surely a reference to Jerusalem, but the New Testament identifies the true or heavenly Jerusalem as the church, whereas the physical city is seen as the dwelling place of spiritual slavery (Gal. 4:21-31; Heb. 12:22-24). This means the final battle is against the church, and not against the nation of Israel at the end of an earthly millennium.

(4) If the millennium (20:1-6) follows the final battle (19:17-21), in which all unbelievers have been completely destroyed, where do the enemy forces come from who fight against Christ at the end of the millennium (20:7-10)?

(5) In 15:1, John states that with the seven plagues or bowl judgments, the wrath of God is finished. In 16:12-16, the sixth bowl judgment concludes with the nations gathered at Armageddon, following which the seventh bowl judgment represents the end of history. It is clear that 19:17-21 picks up the narrative where 16:16 leaves off, and concludes it. This means that 19:17-21 covers the same time frame as the sixth

and seventh bowl judgments, thus bringing to a definitive end the wrath of God against unbelievers. How then could there be a further, much later outpouring of God's wrath related in 20:7-10 when John has told us that wrath is once and for all finished?

(6) According to 20:3, Satan will not be allowed to deceive the nations any longer. It is argued that this refers to his previous deceptive activity during the church age through the beast and false prophet, which is now curtailed in the millennium because of their defeat by Christ in 19:17-21. However, in light of all the other evidence, it is far more likely that this deceptive activity of Satan refers to a much earlier period prior to the beginning of the church age, the period from Babel to Pentecost, the end of which is alluded to in 12:1-9. The title given to Satan in 12:9 ("that ancient serpent, who is called the devil and Satan") reappears in 20:2 ("that ancient serpent, who is the devil and Satan"), and causes us to go back to the previous passage to seek the meaning of the deception and its curtailing. At the cross, Satan thought he had annihilated the Messiah. According to chapter 12, having lost the battle at the resurrection, Satan was thrown out of heaven, with his power (and deceptive ability) curtailed, though not destroyed. *We conclude, therefore, that the "casting down" of the devil to earth in 12:9 and the binding and throwing of the same devil into the abyss of 20:2 are one and the same thing. This binding occurred as a direct result of the resurrection.* This is exactly what Jesus teaches when he speaks of his binding the strong

man through his earthly ministry (Mt. 12:29; Mk. 3:27; Lk. 11:21-22). Ever since the judgment of the nations at Babel, the nations of the world had been handed over to the worship of pagan gods and demonic deception. Beginning at Pentecost, God initiated his plan to reclaim the nations for himself, and he did this by binding the previously unlimited deceiving powers of the devil. During the church age or millennium, Satan is restricted in his previously unlimited ability to deceive the nations, with the result that all those God has chosen can be saved during that period of time. He emerges out of the abyss only at the end of history, to stage one last battle against Christ and his armies, a battle described in 16:12-16, 19:17-21 and 20:7-10.

(7) The judgment of the lake of fire is not initiated until the great white throne judgment of Rev. 20:11-15, which every premillennialist agrees is *following the millennium.* Prior to that, the unsaved dead are held in Hades and the saved are in the Lord's presence (Lk. 23:43; 2 Cor. 5:6; Phil. 1:23; Rev. 7:9-17; 14:1-5). Yet in Rev. 19:19-20, it clearly states that the beast and false prophet were thrown into the lake of fire. Hence, the millennium must have already concluded at the end of chapter 19, for the punishment of the lake of fire has already begun.

Chapter 20 retells the events of the church age from a different perspective, just as the seals, trumpets, visions and bowls already have done. The millennium is another expression for the church age.

CHAPTER EIGHTEEN

GOG, MAGOG AND THE FINAL BATTLE

Dispensational teachers often drag out their maps of the middle east when attempting (once more) to fit Biblical texts into current politics. These maps usually feature the nefarious twins Gog and Magog. Before we try to identify these entities, we need to point out a serious inconsistency in the dispensationalist argument. When the map comes out and the predictions begin, the focus is always on an imminent attack on Israel. Anyone listening would assume that these events are seen as about to unfold. Even during the writing of this book in 2025, dispensationalist teachers appeared online with their maps of Israel surrounded by her enemies, declaring that this may be the end. But *on the dispensationalist's own timeline*, this cannot not the case. Gog and Magog do not appear in the New Testament until Rev. 20:8, which is said by dispensationalists themselves to depict a battle *at the end of the thousand year millennium*. So let's heave a sigh of relief and put those maps away.

The references to these and other nations appear in the prophecies of Ezekiel 38-39. A coalition of peoples is seen by the prophet as attacking Israel. Bear in mind that Ezekiel is prophesying with the raw material he has to hand. His understanding of the Israel of his day is all he has before him. Prophets see armies of horses, not tanks! Ezekiel has no understanding, other than prophetic glimpses, of a much greater plan of God involving his Son and the nations of the world. Ezekiel speaks of a number of nations. The problem is how to identify them. Gog and Magog are variously identified in Jewish literature as Scythia (north of the Black Sea) and Assyria. Ezek. 38:6, 15 simply indicates they come from the far north. Ezek. 38:2 refers to Gog as "prince" (*rosh* in Hebrew, incorrectly identified by dispensationalists as a noun referring to Russia) of Meschech and Tubal. The latter nations (wrongly identified in dispensational literature as Moscow and Tobolsk), were actually peoples of eastern Anatolia (modern day Turkey). The fact that Gog ruled over them tends to place Gog and Magog in the same general geographical area. Ezekiel also speaks of Persia (modern day Iran), Cush and Put (Ethiopia), Gomer (possibly an Iranian tribe which migrated to Turkey) and Beth-togarmah (possibly modern-day Armenia). All the names refer to peoples living on the fringes of the Israelite world. Perhaps the main impression is that these peoples, taken together, come from all parts of the earth.

What is important from our perspective is *how John interprets* this prophetic material. The New Testament understands the prophets from the deeper revelation of the person and work of Christ. We've suggested that the three references in chapters 16, 19 and 20 to the same passages in Ezekiel, and the similar wording in each, indicate that the same battle is referred to in all three texts. Seeing as all interpretive positions agree that the first two references describe a battle at the end of the church age, so must also the reference in chapter 20.

Let's see how John takes the Old Testament texts and interprets them in the light of Christ. The vision John has experienced starting at 20:1 moves to the end of the thousand year period: "And when the thousand years are ended, Satan will be released from his prison and will come out to deceive the nations that are at the four corners of the earth, Gog and Magog, to gather them for battle; their number is like the sand of the sea" (verses 7-8). The "prison" is the same reality referred to as the "bottomless pit" in verses 1-3. Up until this point, Satan has been restricted in his ability to deceive the nations (verse 3), so that the preaching of the Gospel has drawn a response throughout the church age. Now this restraint, in the sovereign purposes of God, has been removed. The result is not only that there is little or no response to the Gospel message, but that the enemy is now able to bring together an army "from the four corners of the earth" to launch a worldwide attack upon the church. The Old Testament background is Ezek. 38:2-7, 39:2, as well as Zechariah chapters 12-14 and Zephaniah chapter 3. All these passages emphasize that God is the ultimate author of this gathering. It is God himself who orchestrates the work of the enemy in bringing the nations together against the worldwide, spiritual Jerusalem of the last days. Although Gog and Magog come from the north, Ezekiel also includes nations of the south in the army (38:5), and John understands this to refer to the nations of the world as a whole, thus demonstrating the scope of the enemy's forces.

The battle comes to its final resolution in verse 9, "And they marched up over the broad plain of the earth and surrounded the camp of the saints and the beloved city, but fire came down from heaven and consumed them." The language is borrowed from Ezekiel, where the worldwide horde "goes up" or "comes up" (38:11, 16) against God's last-days people. The phrase "the camp of the saints" has its roots in Israel's encampments in the wilderness. The wilderness is the place the church is found in, according to 12:6, 14. It is the place of God's spiritual protection. The "camp of the saints," also identified as "the beloved city," describes the worldwide body of Christ. The term "saints" is used in the Old Testament to refer to Israel. In Revelation, however, the word is used 13 times, and always refers to the church (5:8-9; 13:7-10; 14:12, etc.). This again points to the fact that the church is God's last-days covenant people. The fact that the "camp of the saints" is equated with "the beloved city" shows that the city likewise represents the worldwide body of Christ, and is not to be identified with the earthly city of Jerusalem. Rev. 3:12 states that all Christians *of every race and nation* will have the name of this city written on them. The walls and foundations of this city have the names of the twelve tribes and the twelve apostles written on them (21:12-14). This shows it is composed of believers of all ages, including faithful saints of the old covenant. Although the new Jerusalem is an eternal reality, it is also present in an incomplete way now. Paul clearly identifies "the Jerusalem above" with the present-day church (Gal. 4:26), as opposed to "the present Jerusalem" (Gal. 4:25), which is ethnic Israel, pictured as being in slavery. Heb. 12:22 teaches that believers in Christ have already come to "the city of the living God, the heavenly Jerusalem." *Spiritual Jerusalem is the worldwide body of Christ.* The nations of the world, often described in Revelation as led by the "kings of the earth" and empowered by the demonic trinity, attack the church, but "fire came down from heaven and consumed them." They meet the same fate as the armies of Gog in Ezek. 38:22. But the allusion more closely goes back to the story of the soldiers sent to capture Elijah (2 Kgs. 1:10-14). The same story is alluded in in 11:5, where the church is fittingly described as the last-days Elijah.

Now the final act of the battle plays out: "And the devil who had deceived them was thrown into the lake of fire and sulfur where the beast and false prophet were, and they will be tormented day and night forever and ever" (verse 10). These verses are a further account of the events described in 19:17-21. They add the detail that the devil also is thrown into the lake of fire along with the beast and false prophet. There is no verb in Greek — the phrase is literally "where the beast and false prophet." The most natural way of translating is to supply the verb "are" or "were." This makes the point that the devil is cast into the lake of fire not after the beast and false prophet, but at the same time.

This has nothing to do with Russia attacking Israel, either in this age or a thousand years later. It is the worldwide forces of evil conspiring, under satanic leadership, to eradicate the church of Jesus Christ. But as Jesus reminded Peter that day in Galilee, the gates of hell shall not prevail against it.

CHAPTER NINETEEN

ISRAEL AND THE JEWISH PEOPLE IN GOD'S PLAN

God's faithfulness to the Jewish people

"The gifts and the calling of God are irrevocable" (Rom. 11:29). So says Paul in response to the question, "Does God still have a plan for the Jewish people?" In Rom. 1:18-3:20, he has shown that all people are under judgment because of sin, so that possession of the law does not give the Jew any advantage in terms of salvation. During the course of his argument, he stops at 3:1-8 briefly to make the point that this does not cancel the faithfulness of God to the Jews, but he does not elaborate there on what he means by this. From the latter part of chapter 3 to the end of chapter 8, he explains the message of the gospel and its implications for the lives of Christian believers. But the question remains — what then have become of God's promises to Israel? This, of course, was the same question John Nelson Darby was preoccupied with. If God was not faithful to those promises, why should we assume he will be faithful to the promises he has given to the church?

And so in chapters 9-11, Paul develops his answer to the question he briefly introduced in 3:1-8. But unlike Darby, his answer focuses *not on the restoration of the state of Israel but on the restoration of the Jewish people.* In chapters 9 and 10, he describes at length how the Jewish people rejected their Messiah, and how the gospel was received instead by the Gentiles. He shows how Scripture itself prophesies this would happen. After all Paul has said about the disobedience of Israel, he now asks whether this means God has rejected his people (11:1-6). To this the answer is no. God's choice of Paul is itself a demonstration of that (verse 1). If God can save Paul, who was a persecutor of Christians, then there surely must still be hope for other Jews. Therefore, quoting 1 Sam. 12:22, he declares that God "has not rejected his people whom he foreknew" (verse 2a).

The rest of chapter 11 is taken up with Paul's discussion of salvation history. In 11:11-16, he shows how Israel's hardening has resulted in salvation for the Gentiles. The trespass of the Jews has led to the Gentiles being saved (verse 11). But if their failure has meant riches for the Gentiles, how much more powerful will be the impact of their own "inclusion" or "fullness" (verse 12). A time will come when, by contrast with the present season of hardening, the Jews will turn to the Messiah in great numbers or "fullness." This is further defined in verse 15 as the time of their "acceptance" by God, as opposed to the present season of their "rejection." If even the time of their rejection has resulted in reconciliation for the world (the Gentiles coming to Christ), then the time of their acceptance will amount to "life from the dead." In light of this, Paul must warn the Gentile converts against boasting (11:17-22). The Gentiles have been grafted in as wild shoots into the nourishing root of the olive tree, a figure of speech used to describe Israel in the Old Testament (Jer. 11:16-19; Hos. 14:6-7). It is true that some of the natural branches have been removed because of their failure to believe in Christ (verse 17). The olive tree cannot be identified here as national Israel in the same sense it was in the Old Testament, however, because Paul has already spoken of how many of its branches have been cut off — most, in fact. But it does represent the *faithful remnant* descended from the patriarchs, and as such constitutes the original tree into which the Gentile converts have been grafted. The Gentiles have not been grafted into Israel understood as a political state, or even as an ethnic group. They have been grafted into the *faithful remnant* of Israel. The result is the faithful people of God, Jew and Gentile alike. But in this Paul is concerned to make the point that this falling away by most Jews and the grafting in of many Gentiles *does not annul the fact that the olive tree (the faithful Jewish remnant) still exists.* And so the Gentiles must avoid any boasting (verses 18-21).

In 11:23-27, Paul reaches the climax of his message. Israel, as the natural branches, can certainly be grafted back into the natural tree, which is the faithful remnant (verses 23-24). The condition is that they no longer continue in their unbelief. Paul nowhere teaches that any Jewish person can be saved without genuine repentance and faith in the Messiah. But Paul wishes to impart a "mystery" to his Gentile hearers so that they do not become proud (verse 25a). By "mystery" he does not mean some kind of divine riddle beyond human understanding. According to the New Testament, a "mystery" is a secret element in God's plan that was previously hidden but has now been revealed. Paul uses the word in this sense quite often (Rom. 16:25; 1 Cor. 2:1; Eph. 1:9 Col. 1:26; 2 Thess. 2:7; 1 Tim. 3:9). But the mysterious aspect of the plan of God Paul is unveiling in this passage deals with the unfolding of God's plan in history in relation to the Jewish people. The content of the mystery is that Israel's hardening is for a limited period of time, the salvation of the Gentiles will precede the salvation of Israel, and that "all Israel" will eventually be saved (verses 25b-27). He has previously spoken of the future "fullness" of Israel (11:12), of the coming time of their "acceptance" (11:15), and of their being grafted back into their own olive tree (11:24). The "mystery" speaks of a future time in which the Jews, after all their centuries of rejecting the gospel, will unexpectedly turn to the Messiah. *This salvation, however, does not occur outside of faith in that Messiah.*

What is yet to come is that "all Israel" will be saved (verse 26). What does this mean? What is referred to here by "Israel?" Paul says clearly that Christian believers of whatever race are the true Jews (Rom. 2:28-29; Phil. 3:3), the sons and daughters of Abraham (Rom. 4:1-17; Gal. 3:6-9, 26-29) and the Israel of God (Gal. 6:16). The problem, however, is that in verse 25 Paul has clearly referred to ethnic Israel being hardened, and so it is highly likely that when he uses the word "Israel" in the very next verse, the meaning is the same. So "all Israel" in this text must refer to ethnic Jews. Clearly he is referring to a time of great revival among the Jewish people. The period of hardening of the Jews will end when the fullness of the Gentiles has been completed (verse 25). The phrase "all Israel will be saved" refers to a massive turning to Christ among the Jewish people in the very last days before the Lord's return. "All" does not necessarily represent every last Jew living at the time, but that such a great percentage will be saved that an observer could easily say, "All Israel has been saved."

The salvation of Israel at the end of history fulfills God's gracious covenant promises to Abraham, Isaac and Jacob. The Gentiles had in the past been disobedient to God (verse 30), whereas now the Jews are (verse 31a). But the fact that the fullness of the Gentiles has begun to arrive paves the way for God also to move among the Jews (verse 31b). When will this marvelous event taken place? The answer is that the harvest of the Gentiles makes it possible for God to move among the Jews at any time, the same way his return may occur at any time. Apart from the rise of the antichrist and the final rebellion, no other events in redemption history needs to take place before either of these things happen, other than the Gospel going to every people group (Mt. 24:14; Mk. 13:10) in order that the harvest of the Gentiles might be complete. This does not mean we should expect the completion of either harvest to happen soon, just that we should live in light of the fact that it is on the way.

Israel and the promise of the land

Surely, then, we might argue, in view of God's commitment to the Jewish people, he must be equally committed to the Jewish state that was established in 1948? And this is exactly what dispensationalism contends. A key tenet in dispensational theology is the unconditional nature of the land promise to Israel. God's commitment to ethnic Israel includes possession of the land promised to Abraham in perpetuity, and this possession comes to its fulfillment in the modern state of Israel.

But is this the case? Let's step into the panorama of Biblical history and see what we can find.

The land in the Old Testament

From beginning to end, the Bible is the story of God's presence. It begins and ends with a description of God walking back and forth in his dwelling place. It's the story of how that presence was lost and then regained. If we do not understand how we fit into that story and what it implies for our lives, we will have lost track of the Bible's central message, and we will misunderstand the land promise. For a much fuller discussion of this subject, see my book *Israel and the Land Promise in Biblical Prophecy*.

From beginning to end, God's presence is connected with land — a place where God dwells. Eden was a garden temple in which Adam and Eve were placed as priests, with a command to work and keep it safe from evil. But in Gen. 1:28, God gave Adam and Eve a further commission: "And God said to them, 'Be fruitful and multiply and fill the earth and subdue it...'" Not only were they to serve and guard within the garden, they were to extend the boundaries of the garden outward into the inhospitable lands outside — the lands into which they were eventually expelled. God's goal was that the whole creation would be rendered habitable for Adam and his descendants, so that he himself would be glorified throughout his creation as the boundaries of his kingdom were extended and established.

Eden represented the original land promise of God, the place where his kingdom was to be established. The kingdom of God is always connected with land, and it is critical to gain a correct understanding of what that land means in the context of the entire Biblical revelation. The original piece of land was lost through our disobedience, but at that catastrophic moment a prophetic promise came that the seed of the woman would bruise the heel of the serpent. That promise implies the restoration of what was lost, including the land. And if God intended from the beginning that his representatives take possession of all the land represented by the creation, this must also be his ultimate purpose in his restoration of what was lost. The questions we must keep in mind are what is the land, and who is to possess it?

When God judged the nations at Babel and banished them to pagan darkness and the rule of false gods, he chose Abraham to be the founder of a nation he would take for himself (Gen. 12:1-3). A nation cannot exist without either people or land, and God promised Abraham both. At least three times he told Abraham he would give the land to his offspring in perpetuity (12:7; 13:15; 17:8). He told Abraham that his descendants would be innumerable like the stars (Gen. 15:1-6) and that, after a period of four hundred years, his offspring would inherit the land of Canaan (15:18). But the promise is greater than that. God said, "I will surely multiply your offspring as the stars of heaven and as the sand that is on the seashore. And your offspring shall possess the gate of his enemies, and in your offspring shall all the nations of the earth be blessed" (22:17-18). Abraham is to serve as father of a chosen community *by which God will bless all the nations of the world*. The promise cannot be seen in isolation. It stands clearly in the line of the previous commission given to Adam to *fill the earth* with his descendants and extend the boundaries of God's rule. The end goal of God's plan goes far beyond Israel. Israel is the instrument by which God's kingdom is to reach the nations.

The land promise to Abraham was indeed fulfilled through Moses and Joshua, but the land was lost at the exile. The ultimate goal of the land promise, to extend the boundaries of God's rule to the ends of the earth, never came to fruition. But how is this ever to happen when Abraham's descendants turn out not to have the faithfulness of Abraham? Even when Israel returned after the exile, they showed little inclination to obey God, and languished under a succession of foreign rulers. That is why both John the Baptist (Mt. 3:7-10) and Jesus (Jn. 8:39-47) told the Jews they were no children of Abraham at all. So if God has guaranteed fulfillment of the promise to Abraham that through Israel his kingdom rule would come to the nations, God must himself supply a descendant of Abraham who will walk with God in perfect obedience so that the promise is fulfilled. *That descendant is Christ.* He is the one who will fulfill the promises of the covenant that the knowledge of God will come to the nations of the earth. He is the singular, not plural "offspring" to whom the promise comes (Gal. 3:16). And if the land promise is given to Abraham *and his seed* (singular), according to Gen. 12:7; 13:15 and 17:8, then the land promise, according to Gal. 3:16, is ultimately inherited *not by a physical nation* who proved disobedient to the point of rejecting God's Messiah, but by the only perfectly faithful descendant Abraham ever had, Christ himself. How exactly it can be said that the land promise is inherited by Christ we will show in the rest of this chapter.

The highpoint of Israel's history as a nation came during the reigns of David and Solomon. David's reign is pictured as a continuation of the Edenic mandate, for his rule gave his people the seventh day rest (2 Sam. 7:1, 10-11). The land was secure. Not only this, David was a man of God under whose rule high spiritual standards were set in the nation, unlike the old days of idolatry. Yet the events of David's adultery and the subsequent tumult and rebellion in his family showed that all was not well.

The building of the temple under Solomon was a significant advance in the fulfilling of the Edenic mandate. The presence of God, once manifested in the garden, was now again permanently manifested in a physical place. Not only did Solomon extend the boundaries of Israel for the first time to the full extent of what had been promised to Abraham (1 Kgs. 4:24), his fame spread to all nations. Judah and Israel were, in Abrahamic terms, "as many as the sand by the sea," and his wisdom was described as like "sand on the seashore" (1 Kgs.

4:29). Under Solomon, the extension of Eden through the fulfillment of the Abrahamic mandate reached a new high.

Yet all was quickly lost. Following the dedication of the temple (1 Kings 8), Solomon turned away from the Lord (1 Kings 11) and incredibly, in the next 21 chapters, there are only two further references to the temple. Solomon's death was immediately followed by the rebellion of the northern tribes and the dividing of the nation. The glory was gone.

Isaiah begins his book by speaking of the events of the "latter days," when the house of the Lord turns into the highest mountain of the earth. Not only Israel, but all the nations of the earth, will come to this latter-day temple-mountain, and all nations will come under the rule of God (Isa. 2:1-4). When we consider that Ezekiel portrays Eden as a garden-mountain (Ezek. 28:13-14), we realize Isaiah is foreseeing the restoration of Eden. At that time, the "branch" of the Lord, a clearly Messianic figure, will cleanse the faithful remnant, and over Jerusalem the cosmic sign of the Mosaic cloud by day and fire by night will reappear (Isaiah 5). Isaiah ends in the portrayal of an Eden-like garden on a holy mountain called both a new heavens and earth and also a renewed Jerusalem (65:17-22). This land is called Zion and will be "born in one day" (66:8), and to it will come the glory of the nations (66:12), thus fulfilling the Abrahamic promise that in his seed will all the nations of the earth be blessed. A time is coming when God will gather "all nations and tongues" (66:18).

The other prophets bear witness to Isaiah's vision. Jeremiah, like Isaiah, sees a new exodus besides which the original exodus will pale into insignificance (Jer. 16:14-15). This exodus will include people of all nations who seek the Lord (12:14-17). A future repentance of Israel will result in all nations coming to know the Lord and to glory in him (4:1-2). A Davidic king will arise to restore the people and bring them back to the land (Jeremiah 30). This event will occur in the "latter days" (30:24). This inheritance of the land promise is clearly not a reference to return from the Babylonian exile, for it is an exodus worldwide in nature (31:8), *involving all peoples*, not just Jews. In those days God will make a new covenant with his people, not the covenant they broke when they came out of Egypt (31:31-32). His law will be written on their hearts (31:33), a passage Hebrews 8 understands as a reference to the new covenant in Christ. This links the fulfillment of the land promise with Christ, just as in Isaiah.

But Jeremiah goes further. This inheritance of the land promise will involve Jerusalem being rebuilt, never to be overthrown again (31:38-40). God will make an everlasting covenant with his people (32:40), who will be cleansed from sin (33:8), and the city of Jerusalem will be a joy, praise and glory to God before all the nations of the earth (33:9). There can be no doubt fulfillment of the Abrahamic promise is referred to. All this will be accomplished through a righteous branch from the house of David (33:14; see Isa. 11:1-10). Jerusalem, clearly not a reference to the geographical earthly city, will be given a new name, "The Lord is our righteousness" (33:16). David's descendant will initiate an eternal rule (33:17). The new covenant people will be as numerous as the sands of the sea (33:22), thus fulfilling the Edenic mandate and the Abrahamic promise.

The land in the New Testament

And so we come to the New Testament. The mission of Christ, from the very beginning, was the proclamation of the kingdom of God. The kingdom mandate is the fulfillment of the Abrahamic promise, for Jesus will not return until the kingdom has been extended to every people group on earth (Mk. 13:10; Matt. 24:14). The New Testament does not speak much of land in a literal sense, for the same reason that Jesus did not link his ministry to the physical temple or to the physical city of Jerusalem. His kingdom is empowered by the Holy Spirit indwelling his followers, not represented by an earthly ruler sitting on a throne in Jerusalem. The kingdom is fulfilled in two stages: first on earth in a spiritual form, then in the new creation in a literal, physical and geographical form, albeit one transcending the scope of our current cosmos.

The new creation pictured in the last two chapters of the Bible is the ultimate fulfillment of the land promise to Abraham. It represents the triumph of Christ in extending the boundaries of the kingdom where Adam, Noah and Israel had failed. The promise is literally, and not merely spiritually fulfilled, in that the New Testament presents the new creation as a physical reality, unlike pagan concepts of the immaterial afterworld. This new cosmos is related to the old as the resurrection body is to the physical body. It is both a recreation and a renewal. Believers now live in the present reality of a kingdom which has invaded this world, but live also in anticipation of its future fulfillment. That is why the New Testament is not interested in the idea of a land in the order of the old covenant land, but rather looks forward to its eschatological fulfillment in the new creation, which represents the final link in a chain which commences in the garden and concludes in the new Jerusalem.

The land promise to Abraham is a step on the way, but not the final destination. *To see the fulfillment of the land promise in the form of a nation largely composed of non-believers in a geographical location in the middle east is to separate that promise entirely from the work of Christ and thus to diminish it completely.*

In the Sermon on the Mount, Jesus makes the statement, "Blessed are the meek, for they shall inherit the earth" (Matt. 5:5). Here Jesus is quoting Ps. 37:11, "But the meek shall inherit the land." The word "land" in the Psalm is *eretz*, the Hebrew word used in the phrase *eretz Yisrael,* the land of Israel. The Psalm is eschatological in nature, meaning that it speaks of a time in the distant future in which, among other things, the meek shall inherit the land (see verses 18, 29, 34).

The word inherit in Hebrew (*yarash*) is frequently used of Israel inheriting the promised land. Here Jesus takes the land promise and interprets it in light of both the eschatological intent of the Psalm and of his own proclamation of the kingdom of God. He is saying that it is those who follow him who will inherit the Promised Land, *eretz Yisrael*. In making this statement concerning the land, he universalizes it: *it is no longer the land of Israel which is to be inherited, it's the entire earth.* Thus Jesus radically reinterprets the land promise in light of its initial fulfillment in his own ministry.

This theme of rest and inheriting the land reappears in Hebrews. Heb. 4:10 goes back to the rest of Genesis 2 and connects it with the rest through inheritance of the land offered in Deut. 12:8-10. The author, alluding to Numbers 14, points out that the wilderness generation failed to enter that rest through their disobedience. And ultimately, as he and every Jew understood, the rest offered through possession of the land was lost at the exile and never truly regained. But the promise of entering the rest remains (Heb. 4:1), and is possessed not by a latter-days recreated state of Israel consisting largely of those who reject Christ, but rather by all those who do believe in Christ: "For we who have believed enter that rest" (Heb. 4:3). Hebrews draws from this the conclusion that there must be a further rest beyond that promised to the children of Israel represented by the literal promised land.

Paul expands on these themes in various places. As mentioned above, Gen. 12:7 records God's promise to Abraham, "To your offspring I will give this land." This is the original statement of the land promise to Israel, hence a very significant verse. In Gal. 3:16, alluding to this Genesis text, Paul defines the "offspring" or "seed" referred to in the text as Christ. He also references this verse in Rom. 4:13, "The promise to Abraham and his offspring that he would be heir *of the world* did not come through the law but through the righteousness of faith." Notice how Paul makes a significant change in the wording in Genesis, to the effect that Abraham's offspring (Christ) would inherit not the "land" but the "world." This is a legitimate interpretation of Genesis in that the Genesis text also says that in Abraham's seed *all the families of the earth* would be blessed (Gen. 12:3), a theme that is repeated in Gen. 22:18, "And in your offspring shall *all the nations of the earth* be blessed." To reinforce his point, Paul adds the comment in Rom. 4:16 that Abraham is "the father of us all," Jew and Gentile alike, citing Gen. 17:5, "I have made you the father *of many nations*" (Rom. 4:17). It is clear, therefore, that Paul regarded the land promise to Abraham as being fulfilled ultimately not in Israel's possession of Canaan, but rather in Abraham's offspring Christ, and the consequent Gospel expansion of the kingdom of God to every nation.

In Rev. 1:1-3, John has reinterpreted significant passages from Daniel which prophesy a coming kingdom, and has applied them to the church. Daniel had prophesied concerning the rock that would smash every earthly kingdom and fill the earth (Dn. 2:44-45), which he saw as connected with the coming of the Son of Man into the presence of the throne room of God to receive an everlasting kingdom (Dn. 7:9-14), the revelation of which was to be sealed up "until the time of the end" (Dn. 12:4). John uses Daniel's language to announce that these events are now beginning to happen "quickly" or "imminently" (1:1), and that this Son of Man has entered the throne room of God and received his kingdom, the revelation of which is now unsealed (Revelation 5). In Rev. 1:5b-6, this thought is reinforced. John gives praise to Christ: "To him who loves us and has freed us from our sins by his blood and made us a kingdom, priests to his God and Father, to him be glory and dominion forever and ever. Amen." This is a direct reference to Exod. 19:6: "You shall be to me a kingdom of priests and a holy nation." Notice how significant is the change of tense. What was prophesied as future in Exodus and applied to the people of Israel is now stated as an accomplished fact by John and applied to the church. "Kingdom" can mean kingship, royal power, or the exercise of that power. Believers do not merely live within a kingdom, as if the kingdom referred only to a geographical location. Through Christ, they exercise its kingly power. The church is the place where the kingdom power of God operates. The prophesied latter-day kingdom of Daniel has arrived in Christ. The kingdom is the earthly fulfillment of the land promise to Abraham, by which God's rule will be extended to the ends of the earth before Jesus returns (Mt. 24:14; Mk. 13:10). The Exodus passage is quoted again in

5:10, where in the heavenly vision the elders praise the Lamb for making his people "from every tribe and language and people and nation" a "kingdom and priests to our God." And when we come to the end of Revelation, we find that the story line of the Bible ends in the garden temple in which it began. The land lost in Eden is reclaimed in the new Jerusalem. The river, the tree of life, the precious stones and the presence of God which marked the first garden-temple are all there in the second. The only difference is that the presence of evil is banished. The people of every "tribe and language and people and nation" ransomed by the Lamb (Rev. 5:9) represent first, the culmination of the command to be fruitful and multiply; second, the fulfillment of the promise to Abraham that his descendants would possess the nations; and third, the result of the great commission to make disciples of all nations. Revelation 21-22 collapses Ezekiel's vision of the temple, city and land into one city-garden-temple which has expanded to fill the whole creation. The land promise which commenced in the garden, continued in Israel, and reached the nations in the church, finds its eternal fulfillment in its possession of the entire cosmos.

Why would Christians settle for a pale copy which is little more than a return to the covenant which, two thousand years ago, was described as obsolete, growing old and ready to vanish away (Heb. 9:13)? This is not anti-semitic in any sense, for God remains faithful to his promises to the Jewish people. But it is a far greater vision than dispensationalism gives us. Those who see the modern state of Israel as in any sense the fulfillment of Biblical prophecy and not only that, but as having God's unconditional seal of approval, must then endorse a state like any other, one which has had it great moments, and one which has had the opposite. To place divine approval on any human institution is not only foolishness, it is idolatry. The reputation of the church cannot stand or fall on its endorsement of fallible and sinful human beings. The only One worthy of all praise is the One who at this moment sits on the throne of heaven, awaiting the ultimate fulfillment of the land promise.

Soli Deo gloria — glory to God alone.

ABOUT THE AUTHOR

Originally from Toronto, David holds three degrees in theology. He and his wife, Elaine, have planted churches in the UK and Canada. David also teaches internationally in churches, Bible colleges, leadership training centers, and the online platforms TheosUniversity and TheosSeminary. David and Elaine have eight children and ten grandchildren which, let's be honest, is an accomplishment.

NIGHT LIGHT
How to Find God in the Midst of Suffering

By David Campbell

JOY COMES IN THE MORNING. FIND HOPE IN THE NIGHT.

Why are we scared of the dark? Usually it's because we don't know what's there. Perhaps a friend? Perhaps a foe? The Bible tells us that even though we "walk through the valley of the shadow of death," God is with us. In this topical look at Christian suffering, author David Campbell reminds us that God has purpose in every season – even the painful ones. Both provocative and comprehensive, Night Light will give you a foundation of strength

OTHER TITLES BY DAVID CAMPBELL

Exodus
The Road to Freedom in a Deconstructed World

By David Campbell

No Diving
10 Ways to Avoid the Shallow End of your Faith and Go Deeper Into the Bible

By David Campbell

Landmarks
A Comprehensive Look at the Foundations of Faith

By David Campbell

Mystery Explained
A Simple Guide to Revelation

By David Campbell

All titles available from Amazon or see davidhcampbell.com

www.ingramcontent.com/pod-product-compliance
Lightning Source LLC
Chambersburg PA
CBHW071157070526
44584CB00019B/2826